# Democracy's Fourth Wave?

# Oxford Studies in Digital Politics

Series Editor: Andrew Chadwick, Royal Holloway, University of London

# Democracy's Fourth Wave?

DIGITAL MEDIA AND THE ARAB SPRING

PHILIP N. HOWARD

*and*

MUZAMMIL M. HUSSAIN

# OXFORD
## UNIVERSITY PRESS

Oxford University Press is a department of the University of Oxford.
It furthers the University's objective of excellence in research,
scholarship, and education by publishing worldwide.

Oxford    New York
Auckland    Cape Town    Dar es Salaam    Hong Kong    Karachi
Kuala Lumpur    Madrid    Melbourne    Mexico City    Nairobi
New Delhi    Shanghai    Taipei    Toronto

With offices in
Argentina    Austria    Brazil    Chile    Czech Republic    France    Greece
Guatemala    Hungary    Italy    Japan    Poland    Portugal    Singapore
South Korea    Switzerland    Thailand    Turkey    Ukraine    Vietnam

Oxford is a registered trade mark of Oxford University Press
in the UK and certain other countries.

Published in the United States of America by
Oxford University Press
198 Madison Avenue, New York, NY 10016

Library of Congress Cataloging-in-Publication Data
Howard, Philip N.
Democracy's fourth wave? Digital media and the Arab Spring / Philip N. Howard and Muzammil M. Hussain.
p. cm.—(Oxford studies in digital politics)
Includes bibliographical references and index.
ISBN 978-0-19-993697-7 (pbk. : alk. paper)—ISBN 978-0-19-993695-3 (hardcover : alk. paper) 1. Arab Spring,
2010– 2. Information technology—Political aspects—Arab countries 3. Internet—Political aspects—Arab countries.
4. Internet—Social aspects—Arab countries. 5. Revolutions—Arab countries—History—21st century.
6. Arab countries—Politics and government—21st century. I. Hussain, Muzammil M. II. Title.
JQ1850.A91H68    2012
909'.097492708312—dc23    2012023604

Printed in the United States of America
on acid-free paper

*This book is dedicated to those who led and sacrificed for popular democracy.*

# Contents

# List of Figures

# List of Tables

# Acknowledgments

We have received many different kinds of support for this work. This material is based upon work supported by the National Science Foundation under Grant No. 1144286, "RAPID—Social Computing and Political Transition in Tunisia," and Grant No. 0713074, "Human Centered Computing: Information Access, Field Innovation, and Mobile Phone Technologies in Developing Countries." Additional support for case study research came from the US Institutes of Peace under Grant No. 212 11F, "Digital Media, Civic Engagement, and Non-Violent Conflict." Any opinions, findings, and conclusions or recommendations expressed in this material are those of the authors and do not necessarily reflect the views of either the National Science Foundation or US Institutes of Peace. Support for Hussain's fieldwork in Beirut was provided by the Department of Communication at the University of Washington. Support for fieldwork by Howard, Hussain, and other graduate research assistants in Baku, Beirut, Cairo, Gaza, Istanbul, London, Sana'a, and Tunis was provided by the National Science Foundation. This research was conducted with the approval of the university's Human Subjects Division under Applications #32381 and #41115. Within our department, our hardworking chairs Jerry Baldasty and David Domke supported this research through travel funding, coaching on grant writing, and permission to arrange teaching quarters conveniently. A fellowship from Princeton University's Center for Information Technology Policy supported Howard's work on this manuscript.

Some of the material in Chapter 1 has appeared in "The Role of Digital Media," *Journal of Democracy* 22, no. 3 (Howard and Hussain 2011).[1] Some of the material in Chapter 2 appeared as "Opening Closed Regimes: Civil Society, Information Infrastructure, and Political Islam" in *Comparing Digital Politics: Citizen Attitudes and Political Engagement,* edited by Eva Anduiza,

Michael Jensen, and Laia Jorba (Hussain and Howard 2012). Some of the data used in Chapter 4 were also used in "When Do States Disconnect Their Digital Networks?" *Communication Review* 14, no. 2, co-authored with Sheetal Agarwal (Howard, Agarwal, and Hussain 2011). For research assistance, we are grateful to Deen Freelon and Marwa Maziad. For helpful comments and feedback through the writing of this project, Hussain thanks the organizers of talks and workshops by the University of Wisconsin's School of Journalism and Mass Communication, the University of Louisville's Center for Asian Democracy, Uppsala University's Department of Informatics and Media, Harvard and MIT's Truthiness in Digital Media Symposium, and the International Affairs Program at the Lebanese American University. Hussain is grateful for conversations with al-Husein Madhany (Brookings Institution and Doha Network's New Media working group), Jordan Robinson (Silicon Valley Community Foundation), and Farha Tahir (Center for Strategic and International Studies). For helpful comments and feedback, Howard thanks the organizers of talks and workshops by the Freie Universitat Berlin, Radcliffe Institute, Stanford University, and the US Institutes of Peace. Howard is grateful for collegial conversations with Lance Bennett, Dan Chirot, Larry Diamond, Kirsten Foot, Steve Livingston, Joel Migdal, Malcolm Parks, and Gregor Walter-Drop. Howard is also grateful for other conversations with Gina Neff.

The cover photograph was taken on Thursday, 10 February 2011, approximately 100 meters north of the Tahrir Square roundabout, the day President Mubarak enraged Egyptians by publicly refusing to step down. In response, thousands of young people began rapidly organizing for Friday, 11 February 2011, or the infamous "Friday of Departure" that ended with Mubarak's resignation at 6 PM. This image speaks vividly to the intellectual themes of this book, but it also depicts the very real individuals who braved and sacrificed for more. For this photograph, we are grateful to Mr. Alisdare Hickson who endured harassment and detainment along with hundreds more. It is because of these individuals, documenting governmental brutalities and repression directly and intimately, that we have rich stories of victories to celebrate, losses to mourn, and lessons to glean. We have dedicated this book to them.

Philip N. Howard,
Princeton, New Jersey, United States


Muzammil M. Hussain,
Tunis, Tunisia

# Democracy's Fourth Wave?

# Introduction

During the Arab Spring, four of the world's most recalcitrant dictators—Zine el Abadine Ben Ali of Tunisia, Muammar Gaddafi of Libya, Ali Abdullah Saleh of Yemen, and Hosni Mubarak of Egypt—fell after decades in power. Each lost power after unparalleled levels of social protest—and sometimes armed conflict—called for an end to their tough regimes. The "Arab Spring" is what many international commentators are calling the cascading popular democracy movements that began in Tunisia, inspired Egypt, and consequently animated other movements across the region. Several autocrats have had to dismiss their cabinets. Discontent has cascaded over transnational networks of family and friends to Algeria, Jordan, Lebanon, and Yemen. Several countries remain in crisis, and in most of these countries it is not clear if the popular demand for change will result in new sustainable political institutions. Social protests in the Arab world have spread across North Africa and the Middle East, largely because digital media allowed communities to realize that they shared grievances and because they nurtured transportable strategies for mobilizing against dictators. But the early months of the Arab Spring were not about traditional political actors such as unions, political parties, or radical fundamentalists. These protests drew out networks of people, many of whom had not been as successful at political organization before: young entrepreneurs, government workers, women's groups, and the urban middle class.

Ben Ali ruled Tunisia for 20 years, Mubarak reigned in Egypt for 30 years, and Gaddafi held Libya in a tight grip for 40 years. Yet their bravest challengers were 20- and 30-year-olds without ideological baggage, violent intentions, or clear leadership. The groups that initiated and sustained protests had few meaningful experiences with public deliberation or voting and little experience with successful protests. However, these young activists were politically disciplined, pragmatic, and collaborative. Where do young people who grow up in entrenched authoritarian regimes develop political aspirations? How do they learn about political life in other countries where faith and freedom coexist?

The internet, mobile phones, and social networking applications have transformed politics across North Africa and the Middle East. By contextualizing and periodizing the past decade of Arab media systems and information infrastructure development, we can understand how, why, and to what effect this transformation occurred. The contemporary political uses of digital media and information-communication technologies did not erupt in a vacuum. Local and international civil society actors learned to leverage social media while autocratic regimes nurtured information management strategies to control and co-opt these social movements. Digital media use by multiple political actors and interests continue to shape emerging Arab media systems.

Where is social change possible through new communication networks? How have social movements operated across global contexts since the growth of digital media? Since the third wave of democratization, there are few regions with developing societies that remain non-democratic. These include the post-Soviet sphere, some cases in East and Southeast Asia, sub-Saharan Africa, and the Arab Middle East and North Africa. All of these regions have also consistently experienced economic liberalization and adoption of new information infrastructure, both of which have further globalized their societies' interactions with the rest of the world. Of the four regions with persistently non-democratic regimes, the Arab World has the largest number, with the greatest diversity in political culture, media systems, and socioeconomic makeup. What has made possible the rapid mobilization and collective protest action we have witnessed recently? In what ways have ICTs become integrated across the Arab World into the daily lives of its constituents? What role have regimes played in controlling, facilitating, or co-opting new information infrastructures? Last, what role did existing media systems, particularly broadcast networks, serve in connecting and transporting local images and discourses to the rest of the world?

## Civil Society Online

Civil society actors have flourished online, largely because much of the internet's infrastructure is independent of state control. Civil society is often defined as a self-generating and self-supporting community of people who share a normative order and volunteer to organize political, economic, or cultural activities that are independent of the state (Diamond 1994). Civil society groups are a crucial part of all democracies, concerned with public affairs yet autonomous from state bureaucracies so that government policy itself—and government corruption—fall within their purview. Civil society is constituted by a plurality of groups representing diverse perspectives and promoting those perspectives through communications media and cultural institutions. Moreover, a key tenet of the shared normative order is that no one group can claim to represent the whole of society, and that society is best served by a multitude of groups that contribute in different ways to the dissemination and exchange of information about public policy options and national development goals (Diamond 1994).

The importance of the internet for contemporary Arab civil society actors can be attributed to two factors: first, many groups were pushed online because other forms of political communication were inaccessible. Television commercials for advertising to the public were prohibitively expensive and regulated by the state. Radio commercials and newspaper ads were still beyond the budgets of most small civic groups and also similarly regulated by the state. The well-monitored broadcast media were a means by which the state and mainstream political parties regulated discourse. Second, the internet allowed for content to be hosted on servers beyond the control of state censors and afforded anonymity to those who advanced political criticism. During times of crisis, when physical spaces for public conversation and debate closed down, the internet provided virtual spaces for political communication.

Over the last decade, civil society organizations have been pulled online because of the internet's expanding user base and changing demographics of the internet-using population. In part, this was a function of falling costs: in the year 2000, the average resident of Cairo would have spent a quarter of his or her daily income on an hour of internet access at a cyber cafe. By 2010, around 5 percent of the average daily income would buy an hour of access at an internet access point (Howard and World Information Access Project 2007). In Egypt, civil society leaders have used the internet to reach out to foreign and domestic publics, build linkages with like-minded groups, raise funds from group membership, activate support in times of crisis, and provide social services. They also use the internet as a tool for critiquing the government and offering policy alternatives.

Even though a relatively small portion of the general population in these countries has internet access, the portion that is online is politically

Table I.1  **Popular Protests for Democracy in North Africa and the Middle East, 2012, with Minor Political Outcomes**

| Country | Ruler | Years of Rule | Wired Civil Society | Median Age of the Population | Levels of Protest for Popular Democracy and Political Outcomes |
|---|---|---|---|---|---|
| Algeria | Abdelaziz Bouteflika | 12 | Moderate | 28 | 50 casualties or fewer; two-decade state of emergency lifted |
| Djibouti | Ismaël Omar Guelleh | 12 | Small | 21 | 50 casualties or fewer; 300 leaders arrested; election monitors expelled, opposition leaders arrested, no significant victories |
| Iran | Mahmoud Ahmadinejad | 6 | Large | 26 | 50 casualties or fewer; 1,500+ arrests; no significant victories for opposition, government increased digital media censorship (Live, Google, Yahoo, Skype, Mozilla, and others) |
| Iraq | Nouri al-Maliki | 5 | Small | 20 | 50 casualties or fewer, Prime Minister al-Maliki threatened to dismiss poorly performing ministries and hold provincial elections in near future (two years) |
| Lebanon | Michel Sulayman | 3 | Moderate | 30 | 50 casualties or fewer; major resignations of opposition leaders led to governmental collapse |
| Mauritania | Mohamed Ould Abdel Aziz | 2 | Small | 20 | 50 casualties or fewer; 50+ arrested, no significant political victories |

| Country | Leader | | Size | | Details |
|---|---|---|---|---|---|
| Oman | Qaboos bin Said Al Said | 41 | Moderate | 24 | 50 casualties or fewer; 150+ arrested; cabinet reshuffled; increases in student allowances, unemployment benefits, and retirement pensions |
| Palestinian Territories | Ismail Haniya (prime minister); Mahmoud Abbas (president)* | 5 | Large | 18 | 50 casualties or fewer; hundreds injured; major protests [30,000+], Palestine applied for statehood with UN |
| Qatar | Emir Hamad bin Khalifa Al Thani | 16 | Small | 31 | No significant protests; Emir announced elections for Shura Council |
| Somalia | Sharif Sheikh Ahmed | 2 | Moderate | 18 | No significant protests |
| Sudan | Omar al-Bashir | 18 | Large | 19 | 1 death, 70+ arrested, 20+ injuries; president announced that he will not run for 2015 election |
| Syria | Bashar Al-Assad | 11 | Large | 22 | Massive casualties [7,000+], massive injuries [15,000+], massive arrests [70,000+]; emergency law lifted, Supreme State Security Court abolished, tax cuts made, Kurds offered citizenship |
| UAE | Khalifa bin Zayid Al-Nuhayyan | 7 | Moderate | 30 | 5 reform activists arrested, then pardoned |

Source: News Reports during the Arab Spring protests

*Table I.2* **Popular Protests for Democracy in North Africa and the Middle East, 2012, with Major Political Outcomes**

| Country | Ruler | Years of Rule | Wired Civil Society | Median Age of the Population | Levels of Protest for Popular Democracy and Political Outcomes |
|---------|-------|---------------|---------------------|------------------------------|----------------------------------------------------------------|
| Bahrain | Hamad bin Isa Al Khalifa | 12 | Moderate | 31 | Major protests [200,000+] and casualties [50–100], thousands of layoffs, arrests, and instances of torture; major increase in social spending ($2,500+ per family), major suppression of opposition |
| Jordan | Abdullah II bin al-Hussein | 12 | Large | 22 | Major protests [8,000+], some injuries [50–100]; dismissal and replacement of cabinet, $500 million in price cuts and salary increases, Public Gatherings Law reformed to allow unrestricted freedom of expression |
| Kuwait | Sheikh Sabah al-Ahmed al-Jabr al-Sabah | 5 | Small | 30 | 50,000+ protestors; $3,500+ per citizen with free food grant for one year |
| Morocco | Mohammed VI | 12 | Large | 27 | Low casualties [0–50], 150+ injured; commission established to draft new constitution, prime minister given power over cabinet, parliamentary elections held |
| Saudi Arabia | Abdullah bin Abd al-Aziz Al Saud | 6 | Moderate | 25 | 4,000+ protestors offline, 25,000+ online; Low casualties [0–50], 150+ arrests; $90 billion+ announced for public, women to have right to vote in 2015 municipal elections |

| | | | | | |
|---|---|---|---|---|---|
| Syria | Bashar Al-Assad | 11 | Large | 22 | Massive casualties [7,000+], massive injuries [15,000+], massive arrests [70,000+]; emergency law lifted, Supreme State Security Court abolished, tax cuts made, Kurds offered citizenship; over a year of civil war |

*Regime Collapse*

| | | | | | |
|---|---|---|---|---|---|
| Egypt | Hosni Mubarak* | 30 | Large | 24 | 10 million+ protestors; major casualties [1,000+], 6,500+ injured, 12,000+ arrested; ouster and prosecution of Mubarak and resignations of prime ministers Nazif and Shafik, dissolution of parliament, disbanding of state security services and former ruling party |
| Libya | Moammar Gaddafi | 42 | Small | 25 | Civil war and major casualties [7,000+]; eight months of civil war; overthrow of Gaddafi government |
| Tunisia | Zine el Abidine Ben Ali | 24 | Large | 30 | Moderate casualties [200+] and injuries [100+]; ouster of Ben Ali and prime minister, former ruling party disbanded, political prisoners released, democratic elections held |
| Yemen | Ali Abdallah Salih* | 21 | Small | 18 | Major casualties [1,800+], injuries [1,000+], and arrests [1,000+]; major resignations from ruling party and government |

significant. Internet users are very often a developing country's wealthy and educated elites. They tend to be younger and live in capital cities and urban areas, and they tend to be among the most politically active. So the clients for civil society organizations, whether those organizations are faith-based, service oriented, or policy focused, are also potential members and supporters of civic agendas. The proliferation of consumer electronics has made it possible for civic leaders to reach new audiences, but this trend has also empowered local civil society "startups" to launch both small, permanent civic organizations and local, issue-specific campaigns. For example, online civil society was vibrant but constrained in Egypt, but growing and co-opted in Saudi Arabia.

## Comparing Experiences across the Arab Spring

A focused, comparative analysis must take care to define the cases that are in the comparative set and to explain why some are out. In this cross-case, event-driven analysis, we look at the role of digital media in popular movements for democracy that have posed significant challenges to authoritarian rule in North Africa and the Middle East since early 2011. Indeed, we argue that the comparative method is the best approach to understanding the diverse, but still shared, experiences that Arab communities in the region have had with digital media and political change.

Activists around the world saw the creative ways in which protesters in North Africa and the Middle East used digital media, and other researchers have posited links between that region and subsequent protests in Spain, the United Kingdom, China, and elsewhere, including the global "Occupy" movement. So it is plausible that activist strategies and inspirations resonated beyond North Africa and the Middle East. But for the purpose of this comparative work we exclude these cases and focus on the Arab countries in North Africa and the Middle East. Tables I.1 and I.2 identify the countries studied in forthcoming chapters, with details about social movement activities. They are organized by their political outcomes.

Within these countries are a common set of languages, similar if not shared media systems, consistently authoritarian regimes, and rapidly increasing levels of technology diffusion. Palestinian frustration was directed at Israel, not the territorial government. Qatar had no major protests, but the government made concessions preemptively. The political opposition in Iran did mobilize during the Arab Spring, but with less success than achieved during election protests in the summer of 2009. Despite the obvious diversity of these countries, three attributes make all 23 countries a useful comparison set: most of the countries have been slow to democratize, compared to the rest of the developing world; most of these countries have more rapid rates of technology diffusion than the rest of the world; and social elites in nearly all these countries use technologies to censor political culture and manage information flows in ways not often tolerated in the rest of the developing world, but with varying sophistication and success.

Furthermore, there are several modular political phenomena across nations with significant Arab populations: political action is largely based on the emulation of successful examples from others. This occurs through policy imitation and coordination among several Arab countries, especially with regard to telecommunications standards, technology-led economic development, and internet censorship. For several decades, interior ministers of Arab countries have held an annual conference to discuss successful ways of securing their regimes, and in recent years their agenda has extended to the best ways of handling media and internet censorship. But such imitation also occurs among communities of social elites and the leadership of democratization movements. As will be demonstrated in the chapters ahead, ruling elites learn about and imitate the successful strategies of their autocratic neighbors. At the same time, successful democratization strategies are sometimes transported into the collective action strategies of movements in other countries. Through regionalized processes of elite learning and defection, Arab countries seem to democratize in similar ways, not necessarily following the recipes for democratization that have been followed in other regions and at other time periods. Across many Arab countries, democratization movements appear to be learning to use information-communication technologies from each other, linking up to share experiences, and transporting successful organizational strategies. Yet these modular political phenomena are not just found among social movements: state bureaucracies learn censorship strategies from each other, political parties in Arab countries learn how to use ICT's from sympathetic parties in other countries, and part-time and full-time journalists learn new online research and publishing strategies from each other.

Second, many Arab countries have shared technology diffusion patterns and similar systems of political communication, which are together distinct from those in other developing countries. Holding economic wealth constant,

Arab countries have among the highest rates of technology adoption in the developing world. Moreover, many Arab governments have responded to the new information technologies in consistent ways: censorship strategies have been developed with similar objectives of cultural control, internet service providers are held legally responsible for the content that flows over their networks, and government agencies work aggressively to support (often "Islamic") cultural content online. There are, of course, interesting differences among the countries that may account for why digital media were important for political mobilization in some places and not others. Some of these countries have significant fuel economies, others do not (rentier states have long been shown to easily subsidize massive welfare and state security organizations to serve regime interests). Some have high levels of digital media use, others do not. The character of authoritarian regimes also varies, with constitutional monarchies, secular regimes, and states with so little capacity to govern that they are not even very good at being authoritarian.

## Causality and Context

In a sense, all methods are comparative. Research that involves large numbers of cases often involves statistical manipulations that are designed to reduce the number of explanatory variables while expanding the population of cases explained. Even individual country case studies involve some general comparisons to neighboring countries or earlier time periods, or involve setting the particular case into sharp relief against global trends. We do not believe it is useful to compare the Arab Spring to the French Revolution or Russian Revolution. Instead, we seek to compare social movement activities and political outcomes within the region, within the current temporalities of technological and technocratic change. In comparative communication research, our goal is to examine media systems, technology diffusion patterns, the political economy of news, journalism cultures, and technology and telecommunications policy (including engineering standards and intellectual property law). The goal of this book is not a general introduction to the Arab Spring, and readers looking for such an introduction might turn to the collection of essays printed by the Council on Foreign Relations or Marc Lynch's well-considered *The Arab Uprising* (Council on Foreign Relations 2011; Lynch 2012). Our book takes a focused look at the role of digital media during the Arab Spring. But making digital media the entry point for an investigation of the causes of the Arab Spring does not mean that we are only interested in the internet, or mobile phones. In fact, studying the media has come to mean understanding a wide range of technological affordances, telecommunications policies, and cultures of use. Our definition of digital media is a deliberately extensive one: digital media consist of (a) the information infrastructure and tools used to produce and distribute content that has individual value but reflects shared values; (b) the content that takes the digital form of personal messages, news, and ideas, that becomes cultural products; and (c) the people, organizations, and industries that produce and consume both the tools and the content (Howard and Parks 2012).

The tendency among pundits and the popular press is either to make strong arguments about how digital media "caused" the Arab Spring or to dismiss even the possibility of such a causal role with passing reference to the difficulty of agreeing on what causality means. Some argue that information technologies may have had a role but that there were more important *singular factors* at play. We believe—and this is the reason for this study—that it makes more sense to look for combinations of causal factors. Sometimes researchers call these conjoined causal explanations, and they allow for both the preservation of some nuance specific to particular cases and the ability to generalize about a causal recipe that may be transportable to other cases. Our goal is not one explanation but a few parsimonious explanations that cover the most cases in the most sensible ways. We are less interested in the philosophical debate about the nature of causality and more interested in the social consequences of technology use that can be observed by studying a few cases in deep ways. We seek to understand the context of political mobilization in a relatively small set of countries in recent years, and we have relatively nuanced research questions. We do not seek to understand whether technology diffusion causes democratization, because there are some obvious differences in country contexts and a range of political outcomes from the Arab Spring. But when did digital media become an important means of social mobilization, and when did digital media use have political consequences? In other words, when were digital media one of the conjoined causal combinations of factors that explained political outcomes, and when were they irrelevant? It may be that the causal combinations vary by country but that the one consistent component is digital media. We address this specific question at length in the conclusion, but after developing our framework and perspective in the preceding chapters.

## Outline of the Book

Our argument proceeds by reviewing what we already know about digital media and social change. Chapter 1 sets the stage for the Arab Spring and provides a narrative that connects online with offline actions, describes practices of technology use and digital storytelling that have diffused across the region, and demonstrates how key political events had technological components and how important technological interventions had political consequences. We also provide a sequence of events during the Arab Spring, highlighting the significant moments at which digital media had a role in the evolution of the revolutions. The goal of this chapter is not to provide the definitive history of these events but to offer a "media history" of the events. Understanding the timeline of events through the lens of digital media is an important first step, and in subsequent chapters we refer to this timeline to demonstrate the larger mechanics of protest organization, regime response, and the political economy of news.

Chapter 2 privileges the stories of civic leaders, bold activists, and regular citizens who risked much to contest authoritarian rule in their respective countries. This chapter celebrates the creative work of small groups of tech-savvy protesters who managed to have a significant impact on the opportunity structure for opposition leaders. But it also critiques their work, identifying some of their failures, uncertain successes, and problematic outcomes.

Chapter 3 works to tell the longer history of digital media and dissent. Many of the countries in this region are notable for not having, in decades, a large public mobilization for democratic change. But these countries have all had political activists and opposition groups. The Arab Spring was not their first attempt at mobilization, nor was it their first attempt to use digital media to awaken public sentiments. But in the spirit of technologically based innovation, many of these contemporary successes were beta versions of past failures and lessons learned. The Arab Spring may have been their most successful effort to date to use digital media to rally public support, but this chapter serves to set the context preceding the events of early 2011—especially also to highlight how strategies and challenges may evolve in the future.

Subsequently, Chapter 4 investigates the response of authoritarian regimes. During the heady weeks of protest, authoritarian governments responded sometimes with concessions, and then sometimes with violent crackdowns. But every single government that faced public protest, regardless of regime type, had some kind of digital-response strategy. There was a range of responses, some more sophisticated than others, and we explore which, to what effect, and why.

Chapter 5 is about Al Jazeera and the changing political economy of news in the region. Social media and consumer electronics have wrought havoc on news markets, and indeed the relationship between news consumer and news producer is now blurred. Al Jazeera became one of the most innovative news agencies during the Arab Spring, using social media to disseminate fresh content to the rest of the world and bringing feedback from outsiders to desperate activists. This chapter demonstrates how, at key moments, the social media strategy of Al Jazeera not only raised its profile as a credible news organization but also increased its clout as a political actor in the domestic game of opinion formation in several parts of the region.

The final chapter offers a conservative list of the conclusions we can make about the role of digital media in the Arab Spring, bolstered by a fuzzy-set analysis of the causes and consequences, successes and failures of national uprisings. The Western news media played up technology use in reporting from the region. Bloggers and tech-savvy activists promoted their role in leading popular protest, perhaps obscuring the traditional methods and structures of protest that were at work. But what are the most reasonable things we can conclude by comparing popular protest movements from this moment across several countries? In which countries did digital media have a role in the success of social movement mobilization, and in which countries were social movements successful but not really as a result of technology diffusion? We conclude that certain recipes strongly corroborate the technological conditions under which regimes sustained their durability, particularly their level of censorship sophistication, as well as the presence of key technology factors that assisted the interests of social movements, especially access to mobile telephony.

# 1

# Digital Media and the Arab Spring

It has been 15 years since the last "wave" of democratization. Between 1989 and 1995, many remnants of the Soviet Union and failed authoritarian regimes in other parts of the world turned themselves into variously functional electoral democracies. By 2010, roughly three in every five states held some democratic form (Diamond 2009). Certainly there were also large, important countries that made few efforts at democratization, strategically important states run by hereditary rulers, and other states that seemed to be slipping, sliding, or teetering on the edge of dictatorship. But as a region, North Africa and the Middle East were noticeably devoid of popular democracy movements—until the early months of 2011.

Between January and April 2011, public demand for political reform cascaded from Tunis to Cairo, Sanaa, Amman, and Manama. This inspired people in Casablanca, Damascus, Tripoli, and dozens of other secondary cities to take to the streets to demand change. By May, the political casualties were significant: Tunisia's Zine el Abidine Ben Ali and Egypt's Hosni Mubarak, two of the region's most recalcitrant dictators, were gone; Libya was locked in a civil war; and several constitutional monarchs had sacked their cabinets and committed to constitutional reforms (and some several times over). Governments around the region had sought peace by promising their citizens hundreds of billions of dollars in new spending measures for infrastructure projects, family and unemployment benefits, free or subsidized food, salary increases for civil servants and military personnel, tax cuts, affordable-housing subsidies, and social security programs. Morocco and Saudi Arabia appeared to fend off serious domestic uprisings, but the outcomes for other regimes were far from certain. Democratization movements had existed long before technologies such as mobile phones and the internet came to these countries. But with these technologies, people sharing an interest in democracy built extensive networks, created social capital, and organized political action; virtual networks materialized in the streets. Brave citizens made their shared opposition to authoritarian rule known, and digital media helped to accelerate the pace of revolution and build its constituency. Digital media served as an "information equalizer," so described by Seib, allowing for both the telling of compelling stories and the management of all the small communications and logistics tasks that must happen in concert if an uprising is to succeed (Seib 2008).

There are many ways to tell the story of political change. But one of the most consistent narratives from civil society leaders has been that the internet, mobile phones, and applications such as Facebook, Twitter, and other social media made the difference, this time. Digital media provided the important new tools that allowed social movements to accomplish political goals that had previously been unachievable. And judging by the reactions of dictators and other desperate political elites, digital media have become an important part of a modern counterinsurgency strategy. Looking back over the last few months, what concrete things can we say about the role of digital media in political uprisings and democratization during the Arab Spring? What do the events of that time reveal about the contemporary narrative arc of democratization? What implications do the events of the Arab Spring bear for our understanding of how democratization actually works today?

## Tunisian Origins

On December 17, 2010, Mohamed Bouazizi set himself on fire. This young street vendor had tried in vain to fight an inspector's small fine, appealing first to the police, then to municipal authorities, and then to the region's governor. At each appeal he had been physically beaten by security officials. Bruised, humiliated, and frustrated by an unresponsive bureaucracy and thuggish security apparatus, Bouazizi set himself alight in front of the governor's office. By the time he died in a local hospital on January 4, protests had spread to cities throughout the country. It is not enough to say that news of Bouazizi's tragic death traveled quickly, because the state-run media did not cover his death or the simmering hatred in the city of Sidi Bouzid. During those angry weeks in December, it was through blogs and text messages that Tunisians experienced what McAdam has called a "cognitive liberation"; networks of family and friends, feeling sympathy for the dying man's plight, came to realize that they shared common grievances (McAdam 1982). The realization grew as people watched and uploaded YouTube videos about the abusive state, read foreign news coverage of political corruption online, and shared jokes about their aging dictators over the short messaging services (SMS) of mobile phone networks. Through communication networks beyond state control, people crafted strategies for action and a collective goal: to depose their despot.

For many years, the most direct accusations of political corruption had come from the blogosphere ( Jurkiewicz 2010). Pretty much the only investigative journalism into questionable policies and government corruption came from average citizens using the internet in creative ways. Most famous is the graphically simple video of the Tunisian president's plane arriving and leaving Europe's elite shopping destinations with his wife as the only passenger. Following the online publication of this video, the regime vigorously cracked down on YouTube, Facebook, and other online applications. In fact, since 1995 Tunisia has interfered with digital networks for political reasons more times than almost any other state. But a cottage industry of bloggers and activists took to the internet to produce alternative newscasts, create virtual spaces for anonymous conversation about public policy, and commiserate about state persecution. The critics of Ben Ali, president of Tunisia, dominated virtual spaces, but after Bouazizi's death, these critics began occupying public spaces. Shamseddine Abidi, a 29-year-old interior designer, posted regular videos and updates to Facebook, and Al Jazeera used the content to carry news of events to the world. Images of Bouazizi, hospitalized with burns, passed along networks of family and friends, and eventually strangers. An aggressive internet campaign called on fellow citizens and unions to set up committees to support the uprising in Sidi Bouzid. Lawyers and student unions were among the first to move into the streets in an organized way.

The government tried to ban Facebook, Twitter, and video sites such as DailyMotion and YouTube. But within a few days SMS networks were the organizing tool of choice. Less than 20 percent of the overall population actively used social media websites, but almost everyone had access to a mobile phone. Outside the country, the hacker communities of Anonymous and Telecomix helped to cripple government operations with their "Operation Tunisia" denial-of-service attacks, and by building new software to help activists get around state firewalls. The government tried to respond with a counterinsurgency strategy against its tech-savvy opponents, jailing a group of known bloggers in early January. For the most part, however, the political uprising was leaderless in the classical sense—there was no long-standing revolutionary figurehead, traditional opposition leader, or charismatic speechmaker who radicalized the public. But there were prominent nodes in the digital networks, people whose contributions held sway and mobilized turnout. Slim Amamou blogged the revolution (and later took a post in the national unity government and the Arab World's first "Pirate Party"). Sami Ben Gharbia, a Tunisian exile, monitored online censorship attempts and advertised workarounds. "El Général," a middle-class Tunisian rapper, streamed digital "soundtracks for the revolution."

By early January, urgent appeals for help and amateur mobile phone videos were streaming across North Africa. Ben Ali's position seemed precarious. There were major protests in Algeria, along with several additional self-immolations across the region. Again, the state-run news media covered little about events in neighboring Tunisia. The Algerian government tried to block internet access and Facebook use as traffic about public outrage next door increased. But with all the private submarine cables running to Europe, there was no mandatory point of passage for information flows that the Algerian government could shut down. When that government also became a target for the hackers, Anonymous, state information infrastructure suffered. By the time Ben Ali fled Tunisia on January 14, active campaigns for civil disobedience against authoritarian rule were growing in Jordan, Oman, and Yemen. In other countries, such as Lebanon, Mauritania, Saudi Arabia, and Sudan, minor protests erupted on a range of issues and triggered quick concessions or had little impact. But even opposition leaders in these countries drew direct inspiration from what they were tracking in Tunisia. Moreover, opposition leaders across the region were learning the digital tricks for how to catch their ruling elites off guard. Compared to Tunisia, only Egypt's civil society, politically active and cautiously observing developments in Tunisia, was more wired. The stories of success in Tunisia, which soon became more apparent, helped inspire the largest protests in Cairo in 30 years.

## Egypt, Inspired

In Egypt, almost everyone has access to a mobile phone. Overall, the country has the largest internet-using population in the region, second only to that of Iran (although Iran is technically not part of the "Arab World"). This meant that news of Ben Ali's departure spread rapidly through Egypt's social strata. The specific news of his departure was covered, reluctantly, by state-run media. But the same state-run media had been slow to broadcast news of the protests in the region earlier in the month, and parallel protests in Cairo. Like Tunisia,

Egypt has long had a large and active online public sphere. It is here that illegal political parties, radical fundamentalists, investigative journalists, and disaffected citizens interacted. When the Muslim Brotherhood's online news services were banned in Egypt, they moved their server infrastructure to London and kept up their flow of online deliberations and political spin. But it was not the established parties and unions that converted anti-Mubarak vitriol into civil disobedience. It was the campaign to memorialize a murdered blogger.

Wael Ghonim, a regional executive at Google, started the Facebook group, "We are all Khaled Said," to keep alive the memory of a young blogger who had been beaten to death by police for exposing their corruption. Just as digital images of Bouazizi in the hospital passed over networks of family and friends in Egypt, an image of Khaled's bruised face, taken as his body lay in a city morgue, passed from one mobile phone to another, until thousands had seen the picture and were actively developing protest strategies online. And just as videos of a young girl dying in the streets of Tehran had inspired hundreds of thousands of people to take to the streets in the summer of 2009, the webpage to memorialize Said became a portal for collective commiseration. But more than being a digital memorial—Egyptian police have long tormented bloggers—this webpage became a logistical tool and, at least temporarily, a very strong source of community. Ghonim fast became the country's most prominent Tweeter, linking a massive Egyptian social network writing in Arabic with networks of interested English-speaking observers overseas.

The first occupants of Tahrir Square shared many of the hopes and aspirations of their counterparts in Tunis. They were a community of like-minded individuals with similar backgrounds: underemployed, educated, eager for change, but exhausted by the religious fervor and political ideologies of past decades (Bayat 2007). They found solidarity through digital media and used their mobile phones to call their social networks into the streets. Protests escalated quickly. Both government analysts and outsiders were surprised that such a large network of relatively liberal, middle class, peaceful citizens would mobilize against Mubarak so rapidly. The traditional Islamists, opposition parties, and union organizations were there, but liberal and civil society voices dominated the digital conversation about events and the public stages in squares around Cairo during the igniting phases. News and speeches from Mubarak, Obama, and regional leaders were streamed live to phones and laptops throughout the square.

Mubarak tried to disconnect his citizens from the global information infrastructure in the last week of January. It was a desperate maneuver with mixed impact. A small group of tech-savvy students and civil society leaders had organized satellite phones and dial-up connections to Israel and Europe, so they were able to keep up strong links to the rest of the world. And it appears that some of the telecommunications engineers acted slowly on the order to choke off internet access. The first large internet service provider was asked to shut down on Friday, January 28, but engineers didn't get to it until Saturday. Other providers responded quickly but returned to normal service on Monday. The amount of bandwidth going into Egypt certainly dropped off for four days, but it was not the information blackout Mubarak had asked for. Taking down the nation's information infrastructure also crippled government agencies. The people most affected were middle-class Egyptians, who were cut off from internet service at home. Some people stayed there, isolated and uncertain about the status of their friends and family. But in the absence of information about the crisis, others took to the streets, eager to learn what was going on.

A few days later, the Egyptian security services began using Facebook and Twitter as a source of information for a counterinsurgency strategy. They used social media alerts to anticipate the movements of individual activists. They abducted Ghonim once his Facebook group topped 300,000 people (it is now well over 2 million). Digital media helped afford not only a cascade of civil disobedience across the communities living under Egypt's unflappable dictator but it also made for a unique means of civic organization that was observed, modified, and replicated around the region.

## The Digital Contagion of Democracy

Digital media brought the details of social mobilization—and success—against the strongmen of Tunisia and Egypt cascading across the region. Although many analysts did not foresee the Arab Spring, there was evidence that Egypt, Tunisia, and other countries shared features with others that had experienced technology-enabled democratization in recent years (Howard 2010). As images of Bouazizi in the hospital, burned and bandaged, circulated beyond Tunisia, his act of self-immolation inspired similar actions in Algeria, Egypt, Morocco, Mauritania, Jordan, Saudi Arabia, Syria, and Iraq.

As in Tunisia and Egypt, authorities in Algeria, Bahrain, Saudi Arabia, Syria, and Libya tried to stifle digital traffic about the prospects for domestic political change. These governments also actively targeted bloggers for arrest, beatings, and harassment. It is clear that digital media have had an important role in changing the system of political communication during sensitive moments in regime transition. Images of jubilant protesters in Tunisia and Egypt inspired others across the region. Facebook provided an invaluable logistical infrastructure for the initial stages of protest in each country. Text-messaging systems fed people in and outside these countries with information about where the action was, where the abuses were, and what the next steps would be.

Within a few weeks there were widely circulating online tip sheets on how to pull off a successful protest. The *Atlantic Monthly* translated and hosted an "Activist Action Plan," boingboing.net provided guidelines for protecting anonymity online, and Telecomix circulated methods for using landlines to circumvent state blockages of broadband networks. Through Google Earth, Bahrain's Shia population mapped and aggregated photos of the Sunni ruling minority's opulent royal palaces while many people lived in single-room houses with 17-member families. Digital media provided both an awareness of shared grievances and transportable strategies for action.

Prominent human rights blogger Mahmood al-Yousif tweeted during his arrest, instantly linking up the existing networks of local democratization activists such as @OnlineBahrain with international observers through @BahrainRights. In Libya, the first assertion of a competing political authority came online, on a website declaring an alternative government in the form of the Interim Transitional National Council. One of Gaddafi's senior advisors defected by tweeting his resignation and advising Gaddafi to flee.

Algerians with the same levels of dissatisfaction over economic prospects found in Tunisia and Egypt broke out in protest in much the same way. Salima Ghezali, a leading Algerian activist, told Al Jazeera in a phone interview that this outbreak of protest was "both very local and very global." Union-led strikes had been common for decades, but protests of this scale had not occurred since 1991. Algerian protesters were not among the most tech-savvy in the region, but before the country's state-run media reported on local protests or Mubarak's resignation, many residents in Algiers had already received the inspirational news by SMS.

## Digital Contexts, Political Consequences

The range of consequence across Arab regimes and leaders varied widely but were nonetheless severe. Tunisia's Ben Ali and Egypt's Mubarak were removed peacefully, while Libya's Gaddafi was killed by rebel fighters, Yemen's Saleh fled his country, and Syria's Assad has been embattled in a civil war (see Figure 1.1).

*Figure 1.1* Four Dictators—Ben Ali, Saleh, Gaddafi, and Mubarak—before the Arab Spring. (AP Photo/Amr Nabil)

The Algerian government removed its incongruous 19-year state of emergency. Oman's elected legislature got the authority to pass laws. Sudan's war criminal president promised not to seek reelection. All the oil-rich states committed to wealth redistribution or the extension of welfare services.

But real-world politics is not just what happens offline. A classically trained social scientist trying to explain the Arab Spring would point to statistics on the youth bulge, declining economic productivity, rising wealth concentration, high unemployment, and low quality of life. These explanatory factors are often part of the story of social change. It does not diminish their important causal contribution to the Arab Spring to also say that digital media shaped events and outcomes: digital media were singularly powerful in getting out protest messages, in driving the coverage by mainstream broadcasters, in connecting frustrated citizens, and in helping them realize that they shared grievances and could act together to do something about their situation. Indeed, digital media may be among the most proximate of causes because the motivations for protest against authoritarian rule alone had been insufficient for years. It never makes sense to look for simple, solitary causes of revolution. But if the people behind these diverse movements had different reasons to hate their dictators, digital media use may be one of the most consistent parts of the uprising narrative across countries.

Certainly, many journalists have focused on the visible technological tactics that seemed to bring so much success rather than looking at the root causes of social discontent. But this does not mean that information technologies should be excluded from the causal conditions of social discontent. Indeed, social discontent is not just a list of grievances. Collective grievances gestate, and people have to come to agreement on what those grievances are. In the last few years, this gestation process occurred online, particularly in Tunisia, Egypt, and Bahrain. Social discontent took on an organizational form and was ultimately translated online into actionable strategies and achievable goals. In the last few months, this translation process has occurred over mobile phones and social-networking applications, even in countries that are usually very good at co-opting or suppressing opposition, such as Syria, Yemen, and Saudi Arabia.

Indeed, the range of grievances varied significantly from country to country. Dissent existed in these countries long before the internet. But digital media helped turn individualized, localized, and community-specific dissent into a structured movement with a collective consciousness about both shared plights and opportunities for action. It makes more sense to think of conjoined causal combinations: the strength of existing opposition movements, the ability of the regime to buy off opposition leaders, and the use of digital media to build opposition networks. It may be that causal combinations vary but that the one consistent component is digital media.

Broadly speaking, the internet has provided a means and a medium for political resistance across countries. There are several ways in which the new information infrastructure has had an impact on political communication and public opinion formation. These countries, with very different histories and very diverse political cultures, have experienced similar changes to their systems of political communication since the advent of digital technologies. Even though these regimes are very different, we offer propositions about how they have opened up in recent years, largely due to the proliferation of digital and networked information technologies. In most countries where online news use has been surveyed, researchers have found that the number of people who use the internet for political news and information peaks in times of crisis or during elections but that most of the time only a fraction of active internet users regularly consume news.

## Understanding This Wave

It may be premature to call these events a wave of democratization since political outcomes are uncertain and sustainable institutions take years, if not decades, to build. Yet opposition to authoritarian rule was the consistent collective action goal across the region. Social movement leaders actively sought training and advice from the leaders of democratization movements in other countries, and rhetorical appeals for civil liberty appeared consistently from protest to protest. Either way, what are the phases of this latest "wave" of political change?

Looking back over the last 15 years, we can safely say that digital media has—in different ways—become a necessary and sometimes sufficient cause of democratization (Howard 2010). Looking back over the first three months of 2011, there appear to be five phases to the story of digital media and the Arab Spring: The first is a *preparation* phase that involves activists using digital media in creative ways to find each other, build solidarity around shared grievances, and identify collective political goals. The *ignition* phase that follows involves some inciting incident, ignored by the mainstream state-controlled media, that circulates digitally and enrages the public. Next comes a phase of *street protests* that are coordinated digitally. A phase of *international buy-in*, during which digital media are used to draw in international governments, global diasporas, and especially overseas news agencies is next. This all culminates in a *climax* phase in which the state either cracks down and protesters are forced to go home (Bahrain, Iran), rulers concede and meet public demands (Egypt, Tunisia), or groups reach a protracted stalemate (Libya, Syria) and a final denouement of post-protest information in an ideological war between the winners and losers of any resulting social change.

Across the region, the buildup to political upheaval involved the erosion of regime credibility through investigative research into corrupt practices. For most of the constitutional monarchies, military rulers, and strongmen of the region, the internet is the only place to find their critics. Blogs, news organization websites, Twitter feeds, and political listservs are where many women debate on equal footing with men, where policy alternatives are discussed, and where regime secrets are exposed. The buildup to the physical occupation of a central square is actually a fairly quiet process of proliferating mobile phones and internet access. The arrival of new digital technologies becomes an occasion for restructuring the way individuals produce and consume content, so that when a political crisis is ignited, the new habits of technology use are already in place. Many authoritarian governments use some form of social network strategy to surveil their public—Libya's Jamahiriya domestic surveillance committees involved between 10 and 20 percent of the population (Bureau of Democracy, Human Rights and Labor 2005). As technologies such as mobile phones and the internet proliferated and social media websites drew more users, individuals began to assert greater control over their own social networks.

Since 2000, technology proliferation has been particularly rapid in the Arab world. This has resulted in improved informational literacy, particularly in large cities. More people began to get news from overseas and to reconnect with friends and family abroad. It is not that Tunisians and Egyptians decided to have political protests and turned to digital media for logistical support. They were already a relatively wired population who actively maintained their social networks with digital media and then turned to the media they knew best to organize protest. Digital media became a proximate cause of political revolution precisely *because* a significant community of users was already comfortable using digital media before the crisis began. It may seem that digital media use in times of political crisis is new. But for the residents of Tunis, Cairo, and other capitals, it is the everydayness of mobile phones that makes the technology a proximate cause of revolution.

Still, modern democratic activists do get formally trained in working with consumer electronics. Recently, the US Congress approved $30 million to the US Department of State to train more than 5,000 digital activists around the world (Gaouette and Greeley 2011), and the Dutch Foreign Ministry has promised another €6 million, while other Western democratic governments are following suit. General "how-to" websites have become useful resources for activist guides, like "How to Set Up a Dial-up Server." The Alliance of Youth Movements developed a timely list of activities that sympathetic publics abroad could participate in to help Egyptians connect. There were guides to launching a local Facebook protest and sharing images, helping Egyptians dial up through Telecomix, redirecting Egyptian ham-radio signals to Twitter, running relays to increase activists' anonymity, or petitioning Vodafone to reopen their mobile networks in Egypt.

The ignition of popular protest is often a few specific acts of violence, carried out by security services, which are captured and memorialized online but ignored in state-run broadcast media. Much thought goes into choosing the day for rhetorically useful events. These deliberations happen online. There is an incident that is usually not covered by the mainstream broadcast media.

But it is covered by participants who generate their own buzz through digital media. In Tunisia, the inciting incident was not just Bouazizi's self-immolation. In Egypt it was not just Khaled Said's death, or the inspiring success of protest in Tunisia. It was the participatory creation of news and discussion about these events by networks of family, friends, and then strangers when the state-run broadcast media did not air coverage of such activism. When Al Jazeera did not cover the digital activism in Syria, civic leaders there lobbied to have it covered. Al Jazeera produced a long documentary and featured Syrian activist content on its website. Consequently, interest in Syria's opposition movement—both within the country and across the region—grew rapidly.

Oddly enough, the ignition of social protest in this latest wave of political upheaval does not seem to come with recognizable leaders. Charismatic ideologues, labor leaders, religious spokespeople, and eloquent nationalists were noticeably absent in the first days of uprisings. For Tunisia, the ignition of civic discontent was likely Bouazizi's suicide. For Egypt, the eruption of collective dissatisfaction was probably the brazen example of Tunisian citizens and their ultimate success, inspiration that came over digital networks of family and friends from Tunis. For the rest of the region, both countries served as examples of success, stories carried by the digital networks of social media and Al Jazeera. Eventually, formal political actors and public figures joined in.

After ignition, the street battles of political upheaval began, albeit in a unique way. Most of the protests in most of the countries analyzed here were organized in unexpected ways that made it difficult for states to respond. Demonstrators were relatively leaderless and not dominated by unions, existing political parties, clear political ideologies, or religious fervor. The street phase of social protest involved a strategic use of Facebook, Twitter, and other sites to identify the times and locations for civic action. Regimes sometimes adapted to this kind of planning and used the very same social media sites to track who would be mobilizing where or to block particular pages and applications at chosen moments. Syria has blocked Facebook and Twitter on and off since 2007, but the government opened access in the midst of political protest, possibly as a way of tracking and entrapping activists.

Activists were well aware of state-surveillance efforts, directing each other to email, and urging one another not to post sensitive organizational details publicly on Facebook and Twitter. When the Libyan government blocked Facebook, activists took to Muslim dating websites and used the romantic language of courtship and dates to mask their planning for face-to-face meetings and protests. When state officials in Syria started spreading misinformation over Twitter, activists used Google Maps to self-monitor and verify trusted sources. More often than not, the state simply mismanaged information technologies in ways that allowed savvy activists to perform creative workarounds. Mubarak disabled Egypt's broadband infrastructure but left satellite and landline links alone. Gaddafi tried to disable his country's mobile phone networks, but with multiple decentralized home-location registers—including a key node in the eastern city of Benghazi—rebels were able to reinstate the national registry showing which phone numbers linked to which phones.

News coverage of events in the region regularly revealed citizens using their mobile phone cameras to document events—especially their own participation. In Tahrir Square, tank commanders took photos of the crowds and shared them on their social networks. The occupants of Tahrir Square took photos of the tanks, too. When army vehicles were abandoned, people took pictures of themselves in the vehicles for their Facebook pages. People who were arrested took pictures of themselves in custody. Some Egyptians openly speculated that the reason the army did not systematically act against protesters was because soldiers knew they were being constantly photographed and were suddenly aware of their socially proximate connection to the occupants of the square. In countries where the army was ordered to respond more aggressively, the carnage was still documented. YouTube had to develop a special waiver to its usual policy of not publicizing culturally offensive gore to allow the shocking user content being submitted by users in the field of action to go live.

Contemporary political opposition must eventually take the step of seeking international buy-in, and this, too, has become a digitally mediated process. Domestic turmoil can eventually capture international attention. Of course, the degree to which a popular uprising finds an international audience depends on the strategic relationship with the West and also on the proximity of social media networks. Most technology users do not have the sophistication to work around state firewalls or keep up anonymous and confidential communications online. But in each country, a handful of tech-savvy students and civil society leaders do have these skills, and they used them well during the Arab Spring. Learning from other democracy activists elsewhere, these information brokers used satellite phones, direct landline connections to internet service providers (ISPs) in Israel and Europe, and a suite of anonymization software tools to supply the international media with pictures of events on the ground, even when desperate dictators attempted to shut down national ISPs.

The political climax of uprising takes the form of state crackdowns or major concessions to popular demands that can include executive turnover. Stalemates between protesters and ruling elites can result in protracted battles. But in each country, the political climax of uprising can also be marked by a clumsy attempt by the state to disconnect its own people from digital communications networks. Banning access to social media websites, powering down mobile phone towers, and disconnecting internet exchange points in major cities are the desperate strategies an authoritarian government uses for reasserting control. And there are serious economic consequences to disconnecting a nation from global information infrastructures, even temporarily. Interrupting digital services cost Egypt's economy at least $90 million and damaged the country's reputation among technology firms as a stable place for investment. In Tunisia it was activist hackers— "hacktivists"—who did the most economic damage by taking down the stock exchange.

Counterinsurgency campaigns have digital components: by the end of April, activists in Bahrain, Morocco, and Syria had battled to dominate their country's Twitter hashtags, which pro-regime advocates used to push out links to photographs of national monuments and soccer statistics. During critical moments, it can be difficult to tell whether the regime is shutting down mobile phone networks or if digital switches are just being jammed from high use by overworked systems. In either case, the peak moments of crisis are marked by exceptionally poor connectivity—through crushing demand or regime interference. In many of these telecommunications markets, the outcomes are the same: regimes crack down on the largest providers; demand peaks and is rerouted to the few small available digital switches. States either crack down successfully; protesters and elites reach a stalemate with protracted, digital battles; or rulers concede and meet public demands.

Whether the state crackdown sends people home or the protesters send a dictator packing, there is a post-protest information war. Once Mubarak left, the State Security Investigative Service, Egypt's security service, did its best to destroy its organizational archives, though some records leaked online. The websites of activists became portals for constant critique of whoever led the temporary or transitional government. Losers, whether elites or activists, were driven offline and their content became more difficult to find. Outsiders were quickly called to task for the side they took or their opinions on the future. When US Secretary of State Hillary Clinton was booked for a web chat with a popular Egyptian website, 6,500 questions were submitted in two days. By the time the protests were over, a few of the digerati found that they had become newly prominent political figures.

Traditional media sources have also had an important role in the Arab Spring. A key feature of authoritarian rule is that dictators appoint news editors. During the days of uncertainty in Egypt, Mubarak and his information minister, Anas el-Fiqqi, called television anchors personally to berate them for unflattering coverage. And satellite television has done much to create a strong sense of transnational identity in the region. Of the existing news media organizations, Al Jazeera was certainly the most influential because it was the most high-profile regional source of news. For example, Al Jazeera's Dima Khatib was the most prominent commentator on Tunisia when the country erupted, and she served as a key information broker for the revolution through Twitter. Al Jazeera had an exceptionally innovative new media team that converted its traditional news product for use on social media sites and made good use of the existing social networks of its online users. But a key aspect of its success was its use of digital media to collect information and images from countries where its journalists had been harassed or banned. These digital networks gave Al Jazeera's journalists access to more sources and a second life to their news products. Indeed, the actual use of social media has become a news peg, with analysts eager to play with the meme of technology-induced political change.

Regime responses vary in sophistication but often seem several paces behind civil society in terms of technology use. In February, during one of his televised speeches, Muammar Gaddafi lost his train of thought when an aide drew his attention to real-time coverage of his rant. Gaddafi had simply never encountered such instant feedback from a source that could not easily be silenced or punished. Now that protests are dying down in Bahrain, the regime knows where the security holes in its telecommunications network lie. Saudi Arabia has bolstered its server infrastructure so that all traffic flows through internet-exchange points in Riyadh, and online content is monitored closely through censorship software and crowd-sourced monitoring.

It is a mistake to build a theory of democratization around a particular kind of software, a single website, or one piece of hardware. It is also erroneous to label these social events Twitter, Facebook, or Wikileaks Revolutions (Dickinson 2011; Sullivan 2011; Taylor 2011). It does not make sense to argue that digital media cause civil society leaders or dictators to be more effective at their work. Technology tools and the social actors who use them, together, make or suppress political uprising.

# Conclusion: Information Infrastructure and Civil Society

Digital media have changed the tactics for democratization movements and new information and communication technologies played a major role in the Arab Spring. We do not know how the new states in North Africa and the Middle East will stabilize and whether change will come to the remaining, more recalcitrant authoritarian governments. But the consistent narrative arc of the uprisings in the Arab Spring involved digital media intimately. The countries that have experienced the most dramatic political protests are among the most wired in the region and have large, tech-savvy, civil society groups. The countries with the most tech-savvy civil society groups, such as Tunisia and Egypt, removed their dictators with few casualties, while the countries with the weakest technology infrastructure, such as Libya, Syria, and Yemen, were locked in protracted civil wars. As Salamey and Pearson argue, advancements in communications technology and economic globalization have undermined long-standing national authoritarianism in favor of Middle Eastern civil rights and civil society movements (Salamey and Pearson 2012).

In times of political crisis, technology firms sometimes act constructively to either serve the public or capture market share. For example, Google rushed its launch of Speak2Tweet, an application that bypassed Mubarak's attempt to block Twitter use by translating phone messages into text messages. Several tech firms built dedicated portals to allow in-country users to share content. But as Morozov points out, information technologies—and the businesses designing them—do not always support democratization movements (Morozov 2011). Opposition leaders in countries where political parties are illegal sometimes use pseudonyms to avoid government harassment. But doing so on Facebook is a violation of the company's user agreement, and so the company actually shut down some of the protest-group pages. Supporters eventually were successful in having the pages reinstated, but these incidents demonstrated that businesses such as Facebook, YouTube, and Twitter failed to fully appreciate how their users were treating these tools—as public information infrastructure and not just as cool new business applications. Alternately, Google has signed the Global Network Initiative—a compact for preventing web censorship by authoritarian governments; Facebook's commitment is less resolute and maintains only an observer status. It might be technically possible to require Facebook users in Western countries to use real identities but then to also offer levels of anonymity to people living in dictatorships, but no such features or coordinated frameworks exist.

It is difficult to say whether the revolutions would or would not have happened without digital media. We know the region has long had democratic activists—they just have not had many successful protests until now. Radio and television reaches most people, while only 10–20 percent of the population of most countries in the region has easy access to the internet. Yet this subset of people is an important one: it is usually a cluster of government workers, educated professionals, young entrepreneurs, and urban dwellers. These are the networks of people who initiated, coordinated, and sustained civil disobedience. We also know that the countries with the lowest levels of technology proliferation are among those with the weakest democratization movements. Counterfactual scenarios can be intellectually interesting, but the overwhelming evidence about what did happen in a concrete set of cases should probably not be evaluated equally with hypothetical cases and imagined alternative scenarios. Counterfactuals and thought experiments can be fun to work with, but prominence should always be given to the evidence and the patterns in political change for which there are real cases.

It may seem premature to think of this as a wave of democratization, since several states are still in crisis. Democratization waves are measured in years, not months. But like other periods of democratic emergence, the Arab Spring had a unique narrative arc, has involved a particular community of nations, and has caught most autocrats and analysts by surprise. Digital media are important precisely because they had a role in a relatively successful popular mobilization against authoritarian rule. Subsequently, civil society leaders in other countries used digital media in similar ways.

Unlike previous waves of democratization, however, the Arab Spring had several unique features. For the amount of political change that has occurred, there has been limited loss of life. In Algeria, Egypt, Jordan, Morocco, and Tunisia, civil society leaders found that state security services were noticeably more reluctant to move in on protesters precisely because most of the protesters had mobile phone cameras. In Bahrain, Libya, Saudi Arabia, Syria, and Yemen, security services did move on peaceful protests, but good documentation of police abuse made its way to the international community.

For scholars of social movements, collective action, and revolution, there are several things about this latest wave of protests that should challenge our theories of how such protests work. These movements had an unusually distributed leadership. The first days of protest in each country were organized by a core group of literate, middle-class youth who had no particular affinities to nationalism, party, class struggle, or religious fundamentalism. Along with being ideologically mainstream, the core group of organizers did not start their mobilization with something we would recognize as broadcast media. Radio, television, and newspapers have long been part of the narrative of other democratization waves. But here the storyline involves the production and consumption of content over social networks, not the broadcast of ideological frames from a few demagogues to a less-educated public.

Looking over the events of the first months of 2011, we can say more than simply that the internet has changed the way political actors communicate with each other. Since the beginning of the year, social protests in the Arab world have cascaded across North Africa and the Middle East, largely because digital media allowed communities to realize shared grievances and nurture transportable strategies for mobilizing against dictators. In each country, people used digital media to build a political response to a local experience with injustice. They were not inspired by Facebook but by the real tragedies documented on Facebook. Social media have become the scaffolding upon which a functioning civil society can grow, and new information technologies afford activists freedoms they did not have before: information networks not easily controlled by the state and coordination tools that are already embedded in trusted networks of family and friends.

One of the most important reasons for seriously considering the role of information technology during the Arab Spring is that activists and civic leaders themselves say it had a significant impact on their organizational effectiveness. Information infrastructure, according to the stories from across the region, was put to work in the service of political protest. Indeed, the intriguing examples of innovation from the street not only demonstrate how activists did things with technologies that neither engineers nor censors could have predicted. There is also evidence that the organization of protest, the demographic of protesters, and the strategic maneuvers of civic leaders has changed in the digital age.

# 2

## The Recent History of Digital Media and Dissent

Information infrastructure provides new structures for collective action. Since the commercialization of digital media, information infrastructure has become a formative space for nurturing and organizing social action. Such spaces are especially important for the public sphere in non-democratic societies because they can be the *only* public spaces where autonomous—or even anonymous— discussion can take place. Today, in many authoritarian regimes, public opinion forms online. Yet it is a mistake to think that digital media are important simply because they are a new system for quickly delivering content. The longer history of digital media and dissent in the region reveals that the internet, mobile phones, and social media applications are not just content systems; they are referral systems, rating and ranking systems, archiving systems, standard setting systems, deliberative systems, consultative systems, and systems for socialization. In varied ways the many technologies we think of as digital media are sometimes venues for public participation and sometimes means of social control. We identify three periods in which information infrastructure has come to provide new structures for collective action.

For Western media, the role of information technologies in the Arab Spring protests became a common news peg. But such technologies did not arrive suddenly the year before, and the perception that a popular uprising might be successful did not form suddenly. So if we investigate the role of digital media in social change, do we miss the other important, contextual features of each country's domestic politics and international alliances? It would be epistemologically weak to study digital media and expect that our understanding of this factor yields a complete understanding of the whole experience. However, there are things we miss if we do not study the media seriously, and there are reflexive ways of situating media use in larger historical contexts. In other words, digital media provide a useful entry point for understanding how contemporary political communication worked in the regimes that collapsed, and how they worked in the regimes that survived. The system of political communication within the region did change radically with technology diffusion, but this recent history is one of evolution, not revolution.

The internet was privatized in 1995. In the following five years, the internet provided online discussion spaces for political conversations that were not happening offline. Between 2000 and 2006, the political internet expanded with online and alternative news media, which provided what Habermas might recognize as the shared text of a digital public sphere. Since 2007, social media have added the additional dimension of allowing individuals to manage their own social networks, and to push and filter political information along these links to family and friends. Prior to the Arab Spring, past cascades did not have the benefit of commercialized communication networks and technologies, such as social media and mobile telephony, to draw in the wisdom of the crowd and smart mob mobilization. In contrast, the Arab Spring is one of the most impressive examples where laterally organized collective action projects were in combat with vertically organized state bureaucracies.

## Social Movements and Digital Media before the Arab Spring

Prior to the Arab Spring, some countries in the region had vibrant online civil societies where open political conversations took place beyond the control of government censors. In some countries, government censorship was very effective at preventing open political conversations and discouraging the use of digital tools for organizing civil society groups independent of the state. By the end of 2010, the first group of countries was experiencing a significant digital renaissance in how civil society leaders did their work. Protest movements that had organized offline years earlier were starting to organize online, score political victories, and have an influence on public policy. These are also the countries where the contagious digital content of political protest spread most rapidly and where several dictators ultimately lost power. In contrast, by the end of 2010 the second group of countries were experiencing no such renaissance, and while there are a few successful examples of civil society leaders using digital media for political protest, most of the authoritarian governments in these countries were having to spend more and more resources on digital censorship and surveillance to keep ahead of democracy activists.

## Digital Media and the Civic Revival, 1995–2010

Even before their revolutions, Tunisia and Egypt had active blogospheres. Often the most critical coverage of government abuse was done not by newspaper reporters, but by average citizens using their access to the internet in creative ways. Most famous in Tunisia was the graphically simple video of the president's plane arriving and leaving Europe's elite shopping destinations with his wife as the only passenger, mentioned earlier. Since the online publication of that video in August 2007, the regime has variously cracked down on YouTube, Facebook, and other online applications. In Bahrain, it was BahrainOnline.com that attacked the country's prime minister for corruption, but by 2010 every country in the region had an online source for credible information about corruption and regime abuse, spaces for political conversation independent of state control, and social network feeds that distributed news and alternative policy proposals the major news organizations would not carry. Some countries had many such online sources. At first, such content was hosted on purpose-built websites, often with named URLs like BahrainOnline.com. But after 2005, a growing amount of critical content was hosted through social media services; YouTube, DailyMotion, Facebook, and Twitter became portals through which politicized content could be shared. When a regime could not take the criticism, it had to act by blocking access to entire services. For Libyans and Syrians, this content was mostly hosted out of country, though the origin of contributors included both in-country citizens and members of widespread diasporas.

In Egypt, democracy advocates benefited from Cairo's position not only as a cultural hub but also as a media center with a reasonably robust information infrastructure. The diversity in Egypt's media content had long been unusual in the region, and some have argued that because of this the role of digital media in Egypt's uprising may also be unique and not easily compared to other country experiences during the Arab Spring (Khamis 2011). It has enabled the city's politically disaffected but still active youth and others to build a vibrant public sphere online. Over the past several years, political parties and social movements have become particularly adept at using social media to their advantage. The Muslim Brotherhood, for example, used the internet to share information, organize supporters, and conduct other activities that helped it challenge secular authorities. Digital networks are ultimately social networks, so it should not be surprising that the most viral political content actually took the form of music with lyrics that directly targeted political leaders (DeLong-Bas ca. 2011).

In response, the governments of Tunisia and Egypt arrested bloggers, tracked online conversations, and shuttered websites and internet access. In 2005, Egyptian blogger Abdolkarim Nabil Seliman was arrested and imprisoned for four years after criticizing President Hosni Mubarak and the state's religious institutions. In 2007, a number of bloggers were arrested for organizing and covering social protests when the Egyptian parliament approved controversial constitutional amendments. Many activist Egyptian bloggers, some affiliated with groups such as Kefaya and the April 6 Movement, were arrested and faced physical abuse. Egyptian bloggers proved particularly resilient in continuing to publish critical information online, and indeed digital media had for several years provided an opinion platform that neither the state nor traditional political parties could dominate (Dunn 2010; Lim 2012). But in both Tunisia and Egypt a cottage industry of bloggers and activists used the internet to evade government censorship by creating alternative newscasts and building spaces online where individuals could publish information critical of the government without attaching their names to it. Online activists and bloggers, digital news organizations, and political party websites form a virtual ecology of civil society groups that debate contentious issues. In many cases, the boundaries between these organizations are blurred for important reasons. For example, banned political parties, such as Egypt's Muslim Brotherhood, had relied on bloggers who maintained servers located outside the country and thereby could not be taken offline by the government.

Egypt has a number of active political parties, many of which maintain websites and online newsletters to communicate with supporters and constituents, but also with each other. Almost all major parties publish online newspapers, such as the New Wafd Party's *Al Wafd Daily*, the National Progressive Unionist Party's *Al-Ahali* newspaper, the Arab Democratic Nasserist Party's *Al-Arabi* weekly, and the Tomorrow Party's *Al Ghad* weekly. In addition to the discussion spaces fostered by newspapers, party publications like these provide opportunities for cross-party political negotiation. The Muslim Brotherhood had been banned by the government but nonetheless used Arabic and English language publications to maintain a presence in online Egyptian politics equal to—if not more prominent than—that of many politically sanctioned parties.

Before the Arab Spring, Twitter had a loyal following of users in Tunisia and Egypt living mostly in the largest cities. While records of Twitter conversations in both countries prior to the revolutions are not available, in most parts of the world we know that Twitter is used by networks of family and friends to trade jokes and talk about everyday life. Facebook became a political tool because people found it useful for amassing content and building links to like-minded individuals. The Tunisian government was more active than the Egyptian regime in restricting social media. In 2007, for example, it blocked YouTube and DailyMotion for an extended period and in 2008 blocked Facebook for a month. In both cases, observers suspected that the regime was reacting to fears that social media were strengthening the bonds of communication between citizens in ways not easily monitored and managed by the state.

In the hands of average people, digital media became a means of documenting corruption and regime abuses. But it was also a tool for sharing the observations of outsiders. WikiLeaks revealed that the US ambassador to Tunisia had reported that more than half of Tunisia's commercial elites were personally related to President Ben Ali (Anderson 2011). This network was known in the country's diplomatic circles as "the Family," and the ambassador's leaked commentary circulated quickly among regime critiques and embarrassed elites. Yet it was not simply that the networks were exposed online. Information technologies opened the door to new ways of thinking about how to investigate, organize, assemble, and conduct political activities that could be immediately conveyed at a global level (DeLong-Bas ca. 2011).

## Digital Media and Civic Repression, 1995–2010

Heightened levels of political conversation have had several specific consequences for key regimes. The topics of political conversation are rarely unique to digital media, though discussion of electronic surveillance abound on email forums, blogs, and social media feeds. More important, there is a set of political issues that seem to arise consistently across the varied political cultures in which civil society has begun to discuss public policy online. The first topic to arise is often the balance of power and wealth between ruling elites and the rest of the country, or between primary cities, secondary cities, and the countryside, or among ethnic minorities. These conversations are about the relative wealth and impoverishment of some communities and neighborhoods over

others. Discussing and documenting wealth disparities is an especially political act when the ruling elites are from minority communities, or when the
social network of family and business interests that controls wealth is unused
to having its finances tracked. In Egypt, Tunisia, and Syria, the online conversation about who controlled what quickly fed the collective sense of disparity.

Second, complaints about corruption grew louder and more fully substantiated. Through digital media, accusations about graft or abuse became documented in video, audio, and text, and these digital narratives were distributed
over networks of family and friends. In some countries, accusations of official
corruption may have occasionally appeared in the newspaper but only when
the accusations were fully substantiated, regime censors had approved the
coverage, or the target was modest. But digital media allowed the accusations
of human rights abuses, misspent funds, and political favoritism to be more
consistently and systematically documented. Such material became the shared
text of grievances for regime critics.

Third, both the growing conversation about wealth disparities and corruption helped erode the long-held taboo against criticizing leaders directly.
In Tunisia and Egypt, direct criticism of Ben Ali and Mubarak led to arrest
and physical intimidation. In Morocco and Jordan, direct criticism of King
Mohammed VI or King Abdullah was an invitation to the state's security apparatus to take action against the criticizer, and also a violation of a deep-seated
cultural norm that royal figures were the embodiment of the state and beyond
reproach. By 2010, it was increasingly possible to identify, in online news
coverage and political blogs, a Royal's responsibility, negligence, or behavior
relative to policy gaffes.

## Comparing Media Systems

Table 2.1 identifies important points of comparison and divergence in how
digital media have diffused in the countries of North Africa and the Middle
East. As Converse once said of public opinion research, "a sample design
which extracts unrelated individuals from the whole and assigns the opinion of each an equal weight is a travesty on any 'realistic' understanding of
what the concept of public opinion means" (Converse 1987). Today, any
realistic understanding of public opinion formation in Muslim media
systems must come from a critical awareness of the limits to survey data but
also an appreciation that digital-information technologies are providing

new opportunity structures for inclusion in the process of public opinion formation and measurement.

Many scholars have argued that news media are crucial for raising a sense of collective identity (Anderson 1983). And for a long time, social movement theory supposed that revolutions occurred when both the structural opportunities and perceived opportunities for success were necessarily in place. A regime had to be demonstrably fragile and the revolutionaries had to believe they had a chance of achieving their goals. Kurzman argued that the Iranian revolution of 1979 may have been the evidence that perceived opportunities can be a sufficient cause of popular uprising (Kurzman 1996). Different kinds of information technology have long supported discourse and activism in the Muslim communities of the developing world and have often played a role in the political development of secular Islamic states. President Jamal 'Abd al-Nasir skillfully used the radio to strengthen his popular base in Egypt, with emotional appeals that fueled nationalist pride in the 1960s. Iranian revolutionaries used cassette tapes to spread their political messages among networks of students, as have radical Saudi Islamists and Yemeni poets (Fandy 1999; Miller 2007; Sardar 1993; Sreberny-Mohammadi and Mohammadi 1994). Most of the Arab regimes in North Africa and the Middle East had seemed stable and democracy resistant for 40 years (Diamond 2009). The perception that a popular uprising might result in an Arab Spring formed online, but it did not form suddenly.

In the years leading up to the Arab Spring, the diffusion of digital media, in the form of mobile phones, personal computers, and software applications, had a significant impact on the systems of political communication in the countries where civil society was allowed to use such tools and in the countries where governments set the terms of technology access. Egypt's Kefaya Movement started online, but it started in 2004. That the movement began several years prior to the Arab Spring does not undermine the premise that it scored multiple political victories using its online strategies, or that it successfully organized the inciting incidents in Tahrir Square. Digital media did not have, in this way, a "sudden" impact on Egyptian politics. In several countries in the region, it took several years for people with political affinities to find themselves—and each other—online.

In almost every country in the region, mobile phone cameras became small, personal weapons against authoritarian rule. They were not always used as such and the consequences for recording and distributing even fuzzy footage of abusive security services were often severe. Often those who

*Table 2.1*  **The Comparative Context of Digital Media in North Africa and the Middle East**

| | Algeria | Bahrain | Djibouti | Egypt | Iran | Jordan | Kuwait | Lebanon | Libya | Mauritan. |
|---|---|---|---|---|---|---|---|---|---|---|
| *Demographics* | | | | | | | | | | |
| Population[a] | 35 | 0.66 | 0.85 | 80 | 75 | 6.4 | 2.6 | 2.5 | 6.3 | 3.3 |
| Percent Muslim[a] | 98 | 81 | 97 | 95 | 100 | 99 | 86 | 60 | 97 | 99 |
| Literacy,[b] | | | | | | | | | | |
| GDP Per Capita[b] | $6,950 | $35,006 | $2,309 | $6,000 | $10,600 | $5,663 | $37,849 | $15,193 | $16,425 | $2,093 |
| *Political Communication* | | | | | | | | | | |
| Internet Users, 2000[c] | 0 | 6 | 0 | 1 | 0 | 3 | 8 | 8 | 0 | 0 |
| Internet Users, 2010[c] | 13 | 54 | 8 | 15 | 47 | 27 | 42 | 29 | 5 | 2 |
| Mobile Phone Subscriptions, Percent of Inhabitants 2010[c] | 92 | 124 | 19 | 87 | 91 | 107 | 161 | 68 | 172 | 79 |
| Do You Occasionally Use the internet, Percent of Total Population?[d] | .. | .. | .. | 23 (2010) | .. | 32 (2010) | 71 (2007) | 44 (2010) | .. | .. |
| Censorship[e] | | | | | | | | | | |
| Political | N | P | — | N | P | S | S | N | S | — |
| Social | N | P | — | N | P | N | P | N | N | — |
| Conflict/ Security | N | S | — | N | E | N | S | N | N | — |
| Internet Tools | N | E | — | N | P | N | P | N | N | — |

*Note:* In Saudi Arabia, there are multiple mobile phones per person. For Surveillance, N = None, S = Selective, P = Pervasive, E = Extensive.

*Sources:* (a) population, percentage Muslim, and gross domestic product per capita, purchasing power parity in USD in 2009: World Bank, World Development Indicators; (b) percentage of population over 15 who can read and write: CIA World Factbook; (c) internet users as a percentage of total population in 2000: International Telecommunications Union; (d) Pew Global Attitudes Project; (e) OpenNet Initiative.

| | orocco | Oman | Palestinian Territories | Qatar | Saudi Arabia | Somalia | Sudan | Syria | Tunisia | UAE | Yemen |
|---|---|---|---|---|---|---|---|---|---|---|---|
| | 32 | 2.5 | 4.3 | 1.2 | 25 | 9.2 | 31 | 21 | 10.3 | 3.6 | 24 |
| | )0 | 88 | 98 | 78 | 97 | 99 | 71 | 93 | 100 | 76 | 99 |
| | ,754 | $25,301 | — | $88,559 | $20,400 | $600 | $2,300 | $5,208 | $8,536 | $48,821 | $2,598 |
| | 0 | 4 | 1 | 5 | 1 | 0 | 0 | 0 | 1 | 24 | 0 |
| | 41 | 48 | 54 | 67 | 27 | 1 | 9 | 20 | 34 | 69 | 10 |
| | )0 | 166 | — | 132 | 188 | 7 | 41 | 58 | 106 | 145 | 46 |
| | 2 | .. | 48 (2007) | .. | .. | .. | .. | .. | .. | .. | .. |
| | 2007) | | | | | | | | | | |
| | | S | — | S | E | — | S | P | P | E | E |
| | | P | — | P | P | — | E | S | P | P | P |
| | | N | — | S | S | — | N | S | S | S | S |
| | | E | — | P | P | — | E | P | P | P | P |

recorded and distributed mobile phone footage of abusive governments were punished more than the perpetrators of abuse. But even in the toughest authoritarian regimes, there are important examples of how mobile phone cameras were used to document the abuse of power and expose injustice to a broader network. By 2010, most governments in the region had experienced a political controversy of some kind because video evidence they could not control was being accessed online. Second, Al Jazeera became a functionally independent, transnational news medium that generated content even in countries where it was unwelcome. Again, governments did not always respond to the accusations, criticisms, and embarrassing coverage broadcast by Al Jazeera's cable and website feeds. But Al Jazeera clearly rose as a political actor in the region, transforming political discourse by normalizing forms of journalistic content and intellectual critique where challenges to political authority were not only tolerated but encouraged (Lynch 2006). Its markets were not always large, but they were tolerated by some governments.

## Conclusion: Digital Networks as Social Networks

Ruling elites often try to co-opt civil society groups, and in times of political or military crises they can attempt to control the national information infrastructure. But a defining feature of civil society is independence from the authority of the state, even in countries such as Saudi Arabia and Egypt. And in important ways, digital communication networks are also independent of any particular state authority. What has been the impact of digital media on political communication in Arab media systems? How have tools such as mobile phones and the internet affected the process of forming political identity, particularly for the young? When do such tools change the opportunity for civic action, and when do they simply empower ruling elites to be more effective censors?

All in all, information technologies have become a tool for gradually eroding centralized state power. In some countries ruling elites tolerated this erosion, thinking that it would not ultimately threaten their control. In other countries, ruling elites resisted the use of consumer communication electronics through regulation and censorship. But as systems of communication grew, the years leading up to the Arab Spring were notable for a rising number of protests, fomented and organized online but also involving street action. Youth leaders seemed surprised at the speed and size of the civic action they could organize on short notice, and they found themselves drawing international attention and sometimes even scoring small political victories. By 2010, the enemies of the strongmen of Tunisia, Egypt, and Yemen no longer seemed like a fragmented bunch.

In this book, we analyze the best available micro-level data on technology use and changing patterns of political identity and macro-level data on networks of civil society actors. Even though these regimes are very different, we offer four propositions about what has changed since the introduction of new digital communication technologies. First, we argue that citizens in all four countries have been able to greatly increase the level of international news content they can access. Second, a growing portion of the public uses social networking applications in their communications, independent of direct state control. Third, civil society actors have flourished online, even when the state has cracked down domestically. Finally, women and minority movements have been drawn into political discourse online in ways not often available in offline spaces. It is within this context that new forms of social movement organization emerged. In the next chapter we discuss how the diffusion of digital media allowed key civic leaders to develop agile, responsive organizations that were eventually able to outmaneuver authoritarian governments.

# 3

# Information Infrastructure and the Organization of Protest

One of the most important but rarely explored dimensions of digital media and social change is the innovation of new technologies, new applications, and new organizational forms in the lead-up to social protest. Successful activists are exceptionally creative and catch dictators off guard. This chapter provides rich examples of tools and tool kits that civil society leaders now build—sometimes on their own, sometimes with the help of Western digerati and aid agencies—to help organize against political elites. Some of the important innovations are cultural: soundtracks to the revolution produced by digital hip-hop artists from Libya and Algeria inspired young citizens and earned artists jail time. Some of this also involves major states or radical fundamentalists, who redesign technology in ways not expected by engineers to maintain ideological hegemony or promote group propaganda.

No one could have predicted that Mohammed Bouazizi would play a role in unleashing a freedom wave in the Arab world. Yet after the young vegetable merchant stepped in front of a municipal building in Tunisia and set himself on fire in protest of the government in December 2010, democratic fervor spread across North Africa and the Middle East. Governments in Tunisia and Egypt soon fell, civil war broke out in Libya, and protestors took to the streets in Algeria, Morocco, Sudan, Syria, and elsewhere. The Arab Spring had many sources. One of these was social media, which had the power to put a human face on political oppression. Bouazizi's self-immolation was one of several stories told and retold on Facebook, Twitter, and YouTube in ways that inspired dissidents to organize protests, criticize their governments, and spread ideas about democracy. Indeed, Facebook became the information infrastructure that supported political organizing independent not only of the state, but independent of other political parties (Dunn 2010).

# Tunisia and Egypt's Tech-Savvy Popular Democracy Movement

One reason that technology has been an effective tool for democracy advocates in Tunisia and Egypt is that both countries have relatively young, tech-savvy populations. In Tunisia, where the median age is 30, approximately 23 percent of the 10 million people who live there are under the age of 14. In Egypt, where the median age is 24, 33 percent of the country's 83 million inhabitants are under 14. Cell phone use is widespread in both countries, with 93 mobile phone subscribers for every 100 people in Tunisia and 67 mobile phones for every 100 people in Egypt. What's more, in both countries the government has censured the media, giving individuals a strong incentive to turn to the internet for credible sources of information.

Internet use in both countries is also significant. About 25 percent of the population in Tunisia and 10 percent of the population in Egypt has used the internet at least once, with much of the use concentrated among young people. Some 66 percent of the internet-savvy population in Tunisia, and 70 percent in Egypt, is under the age of 34. All of this might explain why many of the people who went into the streets in early 2011 to demonstrate were young, technologically inclined individuals who blogged, Tweeted, or posted to Facebook news events as they unfolded.[1]

In addition to enabling young people to organize, technology has facilitated the growing participation of women in political conversations. Forty-one percent of Tunisia's Facebook population is female; the number is 36 percent for Egypt. More than 30 percent of the Egyptian citizens who took part in street protests were women (Gallup 2012). Women also participated actively in political conversations over Twitter, and they were notably present in street gatherings in both Tunisia and Egypt. Indeed, through social media, women like Esraa Abdel Fattah of the Egyptian Democratic Academy became vocal opponents and thoughtful leaders. Leil-Zahra Mortada's Facebook album of women's involvement in the revolution became a popular site in Egypt.

Our unique dataset of Twitter conversations in Tunisia and Egypt reveals that women were quite active during the uprisings. By distinguishing between people tweeting in-country from those using the same hashtags (key words) but tweeting outside the country, we were able to determine that 30 percent of the people actively contributing to Twitter conversations inside Tunisia were women. Women made up 33 percent of those actively tweeting inside Egypt during the revolution.

# Tunisia—From Oppression to Resistance to Spark for the Region

By early January, protestors' appeals for help and clumsily recorded mobile phone videos were streaming across North Africa, and protests in Algeria and other countries started to crop up. By the time Ben Ali fled Tunisia on January 14, active campaigns for civil disobedience against authoritarian rule were growing in Jordan, Oman, and Yemen. In other countries such as Lebanon, Mauritania, Saudi Arabia, and Sudan, minor protests erupted on a range of issues and triggered quick concessions or had little impact. But even in these countries, opposition leaders appeared to draw inspiration from what they were tracking in Tunisia. Moreover, opposition leaders across the region were learning the digital tricks for how to catch ruling elites off guard. Soon, events in Tunisia would help inspire the largest protests in Cairo in 30 years.

Social media brought a cascade of messages about freedom and democracy across North Africa and the Middle East and helped to raise public expectations for the success of political uprising. Two kinds of evidence reveal much about this cascade: the rhythm of Tweets about political change and the topical evolution of blog posts. The rhythm of tweets is significant because it gives us a window into conversations that took place over the broad digital spectrum. The vast majority of conversations likely involved using cell phones to send text and other types of messages, but there isn't a good database for studying that information. There is, however, a robust set of data for conversations that take place over Twitter, so in a sense Twitter can serve as a proxy for understanding the types of conversations that happened on other forms of digital communication.

And what we can see on Twitter is that a large volume of people—both inside each country and across the globe—were following events as they unfolded. Twitter seems to have been a key tool in the region for raising expectations of success and coordinating strategy. Twitter also seems to have been the key medium for spreading immediate news about big political changes from country to country in the region. As a group, Twitter users are probably more educated and wealthier than the average person and more likely to be found in major cities. They are also, consequently, opinion leaders for whom Twitter served as an important means of carrying on extended conversations about the prospects for liberty and the logistics of social action.

In total, there were 13,262 Tweets using the hashtag most prominently associated with Tunisia's political uprising: #sidibouzid. On average, throughout the study period of January 14 to March 16, 18 percent of tweets about the Tunisian uprising came from inside Tunisia, 8 percent from neighboring countries, and 32 percent from outside the region. The remainder offered no location information. The day Ben Ali resigned, 2,200 tweets from Algeria, Bahrain, Egypt, Morocco, and Yemen concerned the uprising in Tunisia. Many tweets involved personal stories of suffering at the hands of a tough and incompetent regime. Some involved links to critical documentaries on YouTube or made reference to Facebook groups and news stories that did not paint the regime in a flattering light.

With the earliest available records of Twitter feeds, there are clear waves of political consciousness that connect key events, political sentiment, and protestor turnout.[2] In the case of Tunisia, the number of contributions increased steadily between late January and late February. The number of people with no location information also declined, suggesting that as time passed, Tunisians grew more willing to note publicly that they were tweeting from inside Tunisia during the heady days of political change. The flow of content is marked by moments when the service was either overloaded or mobile networks were under attack (or both). Before Ben Ali resigned, more than a thousand people were tweeting each day about political change in Tunisia. Immediately after his resignation, Twitter service declined precipitously, with activists in the country reporting that security forces were interfering with communication networks. When the service returned to normal, Twitter traffic peaked again, with a thousand people in Tunisia tweeting daily and street protests drawing out tens of thousands. This lasted for several weeks, until the last vestiges of the ruling elite were removed from power.

Just as Twitter traffic peaked with street protests, the topics discussed in the Tunisian blogosphere closely tracked with public interest in political freedom. Figure 3.1 tracks four of the most important keywords in the Tunisian blogosphere, in which content is mostly written in French. Analysis of the structure of content and links in the Tunisian blogosphere between November 2010 and May 2011 indicates direct parallels between online political conversations and offline events. Particularly after December 17, 2010, when Bouazizi set himself on fire, the Tunisian blogosphere experienced a spike in the frequency of online conversations about revolution and President Ben Ali's leadership. In this way, the volume of digital conversations peaks with the size of street demonstrations, and the content of these conversations directly reflects public sentiments. Figure 3.1 reveals the rise and fall of certain keywords in the Tunisian blogosphere, beginning two months before the popular uprising.[3]

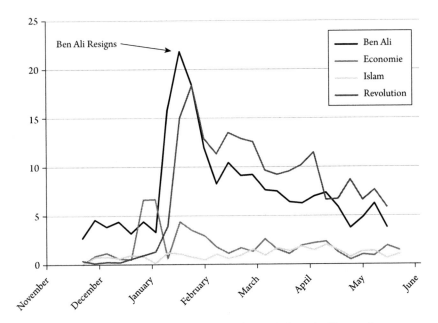

*Figure 3.1* Percentage of Tunisian Blogs with Posts on Politics, by Keyword.
   *Note*: Figure represents the percentage of all blog posts containing at least one of six keywords. Based on data captured through eCairn beginning November 20, 2010.

Tunisian bloggers had, for several years, been among the most critical opponents of Ben Ali's regime. By scanning the structure of content and links of the Tunisian blogosphere, we can chart the progress of the idea of political reform. Many Tunisian bloggers wrote in French and Arabic. Moreover, distinct keywords and themes regarding economic grievances and democratization arose preceding the popular uprising. Among Tunisia's digerati, economic woes and Ben Ali's leadership are key topics from November to December. But with Bouazizi's death in early January came a spike in conversation about his plight and shortly thereafter a growth in the number of conversations about freedom and revolution. Islam, as a political theme, tracks on only a few blogs and the interest in economic issues diminishes over time relative to themes of freedom and revolution.

Talk about revolution continued even after Ben Ali fled the country because his replacement, Mohamed Ghannouchi, was viewed by many as part of the old regime. Consequently, the percentage of blog posts with the keywords "revolution" and "liberty" peaked after Ben Ali had already left office. By the third week of January, 18 percent of all Tunisian blog posts talked about revolution; 10 percent discussed liberty. That week marked the climax of protester turnout with estimates ranging from 40,000 to 100,000 people in the streets. The primary topic of political conversation in Tunisian blogs then became "revolution" until a public rally of at least 100,000 people on February 27, after which Ghannouchi was forced to resign. In Tunisia, the blogosphere anticipated what happened on the ground by days. Demand online for liberty eventually manifested itself in the streets.

The relative prominence of conversations about freedom among Tunisia's wired middle class is consistent with anecdotal evidence of public sentiment during the first few days of the uprising. Journalists and country experts consistently expressed surprise that traditional political ideologies and political parties were absent from the protests. Major opposition parties and political leaders did not feature as prominently as Bouazizi, and were not particularly associated with conversations about liberty or the prospects of revolution. And conversations about liberty and freedom were more important than conversations about Islam.

## Protest Narratives Cascade across the Region

Around the region, people increasingly tweeted about events occurring in their neighborhoods. Stories of success and difficulty spread widely and created a kind of freedom meme. The same meme traveled across the region through Facebook and YouTube, as inspiring images were captured by mobile phone and transmitted. Interestingly, their social media conversations about revolution underwent a linguistic change in keeping with the rising feelings of national and Arabic pride. Prior to the groundswell of support for political change, most of the content about protest coming over social media from users in the region was in English and French. After the inciting incidents in Tunisia and Egypt, most of the content flowed resolutely in Arabic (Mourtada and Salem 2011). In addition, Lotan et al.'s analysis of Twitter contributions (Lotan et al. 2011) reveals a typology of users based on the frequency and form of communication:

- Mainstream media organizations: news and media organizations that have both digital and non-digital outlets (e.g., @AJEnglish, @nytimes).
- Mainstream news media organizations: blogs, news portals, or journalistic entities that exist solely online (e.g., @HuffingtonPost).
- Non-media organizations: groups, companies, or organizations that are not primarily news-oriented (e.g., @Vodafone, @Wikileaks).

- Mainstream media employees: individuals employed by MSM organizations, or who regularly work as freelancers for MSM organizations (e.g., @AndersonCooper).
- Bloggers: individuals who post regularly to an established blog, and who appear to identify as a blogger on Twitter (e.g., @gr33ndata).
- Activists: individuals who self-identify as an activist, who work at an activist organization, or who appear to be tweeting purely about activist topics to capture the attention of others (e.g., @Ghonim).
- Digerati: individuals who have worldwide influence in social media circles and are, thus, widely followed on Twitter (e.g., @TimOReilly).
- Political actors: individuals who are known primarily for their relationship to government (e.g., @Diego_Arria, @JeanMarcAyrault).
- Celebrities: individuals who are famous for reasons unrelated to technology, politics, or activism (e.g., @Alyssa_Milano).
- Researchers: an individual who is affiliated with a university or think tank and whose expertise is focused on Middle East issues (e.g., @abuardvark).
- Bots: accounts that appears to be an automated service tweeting consistent content, usually in extraordinary volumes (e.g., @toptweets).

The content that was flowing over Twitter, for many users in the countries affected by protests, was also of a peculiar kind. Papacharissi and Oliviera call it "affective news" because so much of the content included links to stories tagged by personal content, or personal photos and narrative about events on the ground (Papacharissi and Oliveira 2012).

Here we specifically study tweets, rather than simply Twitter users, because they represent a sense of conversation and active dialogue about freedom that transcended national boundaries. For example, after Egyptians heard that Ben Ali had fled Tunisia on January 14, Twitter user and journalist Gigi Ibrahim declared that "the Tunisian revolution is being twitterized . . . history is being written by the people #sidibouzid #Tunisia." Blogger Tarek Shalaby echoed with, "we will follow it!" On January 25, journalist Hossam el-Hamalawy noted that "tens of thousands r protesting [with] the same chants as the Tunisians." In the aftermath of an unexpectedly large turnout in Egypt that day, Mahmoud Salem—the blogger and activist also known as "Sandmonkey"—urged his Twitter followers to "please remember, it took a month of protests 4 Tunis revolution 2 succeed. Persistence is everything."

Figure 3.2 demonstrates the rising wave of tweets about events in other countries and the prospects of making democratic gains. To produce this

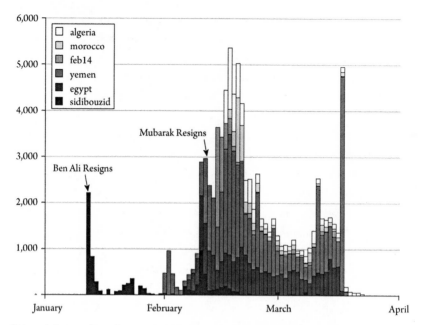

*Figure 3.2* Number of Tweets in the Region Using Hashtags for Neighboring Countries.

Note: These are the hashtags that came to be associated most prominently with political uprisings in Algeria, Egypt, Bahrain, Tunisia, Morocco, and Yemen. The hashtags analyzed, in order, were "#algeria," "#egypt," "#feb14," "#morocco," "#sidibouzid," and "#yemen."

graphic, we first selected all the tweets we could confirm as originating in Algeria, Bahrain, Egypt, Morocco, Tunisia or Yemen using geo-data. We then isolated the tweets using hashtags for countries and freedom movements other than country of origin. In other words, this figure specifically displays the rate at which people in each country caught and transmitted the meme of political freedom from other countries. In the two weeks after Mubarak's resignation, there was an average of 3,400 tweets a day about the political crisis in Egypt by people living in neighboring countries.

Figure 3.2 reveals that at the peak of events in Tunisia, there were 2,200 tweets about Ben Ali's resignation from outside Tunisia (but within the region). In the subsequent months, the hashtags associated with conversations about political change in particular countries were often used by people in neighboring countries. In other words, people in countries throughout the region were drawn into an extended conversation about social uprising. As street protests arose in Tunisia and Egypt, then Yemen and Bahrain, and eventually Algeria and Morocco, people across the region tweeted in real time about big events. This is significant because it reveals how the success of demands for political change in Tunisia and Egypt led individuals in other countries to pick up the conversation and talk about how it was relevant to their own lives. In other words, it helped cascade conversation about freedom across the region.

## Egypt—The Freedom Meme Spreads through Social Networks

News of Ben Ali's departure spread rapidly in Egypt, where almost everyone has access to a mobile phone and the internet-using population is the largest in the Arab world. State-run media in Egypt, which had been slow to report protests in the region and in Cairo, reluctantly covered Ben Ali's exit. The first occupants of Cairo's Tahrir Square shared many of the hopes and aspirations of their counterparts in Tunis. They were a community of like-minded individuals, underemployed, educated, eager for change but not committed to religious fervor or a specific political ideology. They found solidarity through social media, and then used their mobile phones to call their social networks into the street. In a surprise to both government analysts and outsiders, a large network of relatively liberal, middle class, peaceful citizens quickly mobilized against Mubarak. The traditional Islamists, opposition parties, and union organizations were in the square too, but liberal and civil society voices dominated the digital conversation about events.

Events in Egypt not only helped spark protest movements in neighboring countries, they also seeded a global conversation about the politics of freedom. Twitter was used to draw the international community into Egyptian events. Real-time conversations about protester turnout, regime response, and Mubarak's political options did not just occur between Egyptians. Elsewhere, we have found that as domestic and international pressure for Mubarak to resign was building, there was an interesting shift in the geo-data of people tweeting about political change in Egypt. Two weeks prior to his resignation, we find that 34 percent of the tweets on the topic of political change in Egypt were coming from people who self-identified as being outside the region entirely. But as public engagement with political protest grew in the week prior to his resignation, the relative contribution of outsiders dwindled to just 12 percent: in other words, the vast majority of tweets were coming from people who were either in the country or in the region, or had refused to give their location information (a common strategy for political protesters). The regime's interference with digital networks interrupted online traffic on some days.

Yet in-country Twitter traffic peaked on the day street protests reached into the thousands and then peaked again during the last days of Mubarak's hold on power. Over time, the number of Egyptians in Egypt tweeting about politics surpassed the number of individuals tweeting from elsewhere in the region.

## Social Media's Centrality to Political Conversation

Between November 2010 and May 2011, the amount of content produced online by major Egyptian political actors increased significantly as they reacted to events on the street and adjusted strategy to compete for the affinities of newly freed Egyptian voters. Some observers have been skeptical of social media's relevance to the evolution of political conversations in Egypt. But we find that in Egypt, Facebook and Western news media are central to online political discourse. We mapped the digital space in Egypt twice, once in November 2010 and a second time in May 2011. What we found was that Egypt's major political actors often linked to social networking and news services. In fact, major Egyptian political websites were far more likely to link to Facebook or Western media sites like CNN than they were to each other. For Egyptians, Facebook and other social media are not simply sites used for entertainment or managing their personal lives. These social media are where Egyptians go to practice politics. Political parties have learned this over the past few months, and are working hard to put new content online and connect with potential supporters—some of whom may be voters in upcoming elections.

In November 2010, more than 20 percent of the 928 links going out of Egyptian political party websites were to social media sites such as Facebook, YouTube, and Twitter, and to blogging tools or Western news websites such as the BBC or CNN. By May 2011, however, this had dropped to 15 percent of 1,332 outgoing links. Table 3.1 highlights the number of pages, unique external links, and overall size of the websites of major political groups in Egypt, both before the revolution and after. Groups that were unlicensed by Mubarak's government are indicated with an asterisk (*). Both the number of pages and the volume (in megabytes) are good indicators of the overall size of the website, though the first may be a good measure of text content and the second a measure of multimedia content. The number of unique external links is a good indicator of how much a political party connects its ideas and content to larger political conversations. Table 3.1 reveals something about how the structure of political content online changed before and after the popular uprising in Egypt.[4]

*Table 3.1*  **Online Structure of Egyptian Political Parties, Before and After Revolution**

| Political Party, URL | Before Revolution | | | After Revolution | | |
|---|---|---|---|---|---|---|
| | Pages | Unique External Links | Volume (MB) | Pages | Unique External Links | Volume (MB) |
| April 6 Youth Movement, 6april.org | .. | .. | .. | 378 | 8 | 48 |
| Communist Party of Egypt*, cpegypt.tk | 1,297 | 248 | 62 | 3,379 | 9 | 190 |
| Egyptian Greens, egyptiangreens.com | 441 | 2 | 16 | 527 | 2 | 17 |
| Kefaya Movement*, harakamasria.org | 4,372 | 90 | 24 | 4,522 | 78 | 25 |
| National Association for Change*, taghyeer.net | 1,983 | 2 | 35 | .. | .. | .. |
| National Democratic Party, ndp.org.eg | 1,343 | 11 | 43 | .. | .. | .. |
| New Wafd Party, alwafdparty.org | 78 | .. | 9 | 2,015 | 11 | 165 |
| Progressive Nationalist Unionist Party, al-ahaly.com | 1,583 | 12 | 22 | 323 | 7 | 7 |
| Socialist Labour Party, el3amal.net | 304 | 7 | 2 | 615 | 6 | 4 |

(*continued*)

Table 3.1    (continued)

| Political Party, URL | Before Revolution | | | After Revolution | | |
|---|---|---|---|---|---|---|
| | Pages | Unique External Links | Volume (MB) | Pages | Unique External Links | Volume (MB) |
| Muslim Brotherhood (Arabic)*, ikhwanonline.com | 6,123 | 66 | 137 | 7,948 | 67 | 459 |
| Muslim Brotherhood (English)*, ikhwanweb.com | 4,372 | 896 | 196 | 4,579 | 739 | 386 |

Note: Groups marked with an asterisk (*) were illegal political parties until recently. MB refers to megabytes of content.

The network structure of Egypt's online political parties and pressure groups, along with the unique external websites originating from a group's homepage, is mapped in Figures 3.3 and 3.4. The shaded circle around a group's origin node represents the volume of pages within that site (the diameter of each circle directly represents the amount of content, in megabytes, that each site hosts). Comparing the ratio of unique external pages to a site's volume indicates how much any given site is relying on external and self-produced content. In the network map of Egypt's online political sphere, each dot represents an external link originating from the political parties' websites. When two dots connect, it is a site that two parties linked to and any links position political parties closer together based on the program's algorithm. We can see the clear arrangement around blogs and state-run media sites.

In May 2011, Western social media and news outlets were still at the center of the online Egyptian political network. The majority of common links between Egypt's political parties were commercial, Western sites. The most central of these sites were Facebook, Google, YouTube, CNN, Yahoo!, Blogger, BBC, Flickr, Twitter, and Wordpress. Notably, none of the websites crawled in November 2010 linked to Al Jazeera, and there were only six outgoing links to Al Jazeera when the crawl was repeated in May 2011.

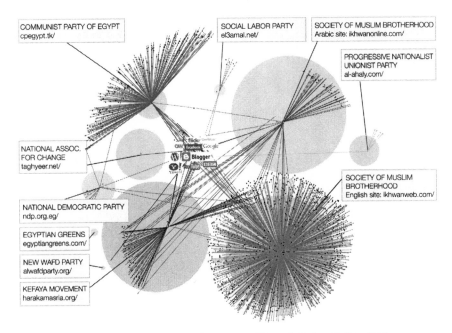

*Figure 3.3* Pre-Uprising Structure and Content of Egypt's Online Political Sphere, November 2010.

*Source:* Howard, Duffy et al. 2011.

The results of the May 2011 network generation show that the same Western media are still present, but are now oriented along the periphery of the Muslim Brotherhood's websites. And while links to Western media are found on many Egyptian sites, the Muslim Brotherhood provides a surprising amount of new content in both its Arabic and English language sites. In terms of pages, the Arabic version grew by almost 60 percent, and in terms of size it more than tripled. Considering how large the Muslim Brotherhood's Arabic language website is, it is interesting to note how relatively few links it made to outside news sources or content from other political actors. The tendency to have active linking within the community with little activity moving outward may indicate that the Muslim Brotherhood relies primarily on digital media for organizational deliberation. Indeed, this organization had an active community of citizen journalists and civic bloggers who were forced to discuss political issues online because of the Mubarak regime's strong offline censorship.

The National Democratic Party's website (ndp.org.eg) is no longer in service. The last publicly available versions of the site were cached in Google's search engine on February 26, 2011. There is no redirect, so it appears that the host servers have been taken offline. The April 6 Movement, which had a

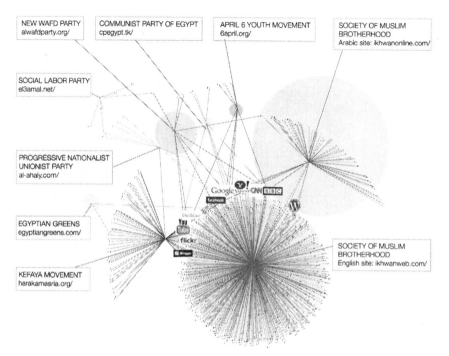

*Figure 3.4*  Post-Uprising Structure and Content of Egypt's Online Political Sphere, May 2011.

Source: Howard, Duffy, et al. 2011

central role in the uprising, barely existed as a standalone URL in November 2010 because most of its content was not on its own website but almost exclusively on social networking platforms like Facebook and Twitter. The National Association for Change and the National Democratic Party ceased to exist after the uprising.

## The Muslim Brotherhood's Changing Online Content

Even today, Facebook remains one of the most central nodes in Egyptian networks of political information. In November 2010, before the political uprising, the websites of major political actors had more links to Facebook and other Western media than they had to each other. By May 2011, Facebook was still central, but with Mubarak's departure, the volume of digital content produced by the Muslim Brotherhood has come to dominate these networks.

The most significant change in how political parties operate online involves two of the websites of the Muslim Brotherhood. In November 2010, these websites had 10,495 pages, with 962 outgoing links and 333 megabytes of content. By May 2011, this had evolved to 12,527 pages, 806 links, and 845 megabytes of content. In other words, the number of web pages had grown by 19 percent, the number of outgoing links had diminished by 16 percent, and the volume of content had ballooned by 154 percent.

The Muslim Brotherhood's presence on English and Arabic websites was dominant in Egypt's online political sphere before the November elections began and has grown significantly since then, particularly with respect to content. The Brotherhood's English site links to much more external content than its Arabic site, but it is a smaller site in terms of hosted content. This may indicate that when seeking to inform their English-speaking audience, the Muslim Brotherhood provides more links to external content to build legitimacy. It may also indicate that there is more English content than Arabic content available to link to. The Arabic version of the site has fewer external links (90 percent fewer) and more hosted content (159 percent more) than the English version.

The Muslim Brotherhood is actively developing its own social media sphere, with ikhwantube.com and ikhwanbook.com—websites that offer much of the functionality of Western namesakes like YouTube and Facebook. As regional experts might expect, the Muslim Brotherhood and Communist Party of Egypt share a number of links to the same kinds of content. Both parties were the major opponents to Mubarak's ruling National Democratic Party. Since the November 2010 elections, both parties have increased the amount of content they have online.

## Streaming Video Made Democratic Aspirations Viral

YouTube became a particularly important tool for spreading news and information of Egypt's uprising around the world. Elsewhere, we identified the top viral videos as of June 2011 (Howard, Duffy et al. 2011). While it is difficult to measure the precise impact of these videos on audiences, some images of suffering certainly would have spurred protests and heightened moral outrage.

The first significant Egyptian video went viral on January 25, 2011. The video depicts thousands of protesters converging on Tahrir Square. The images were captured by an amateur cameraman looking out of a building near the main road. Based on the metadata reported on the uploader's YouTube account, the video was distributed by an account registered as located in the

United States. Since then, this video has accumulated more than 600,000 views. Based on tracking of the embed code, it is most likely that the video received popular attention after being posted on AllMania.com, a sports commentary site that experienced a 600 percent increase in traffic in January 2011.

RussiaToday's YouTube channel contributed five of the top-20 viral videos, totaling 1,200,000 cumulative views. These videos were from citizen journalists and included live footage rebroadcast through the news agency's outlets. Al Jazeera English's YouTube channel similarly contributed three videos, totaling more than 300,000 views. Reuters's YouTube channel contributed one video totaling more than 200,000 views. Between May 16 and 20, 2011, we hand coded the most prominent videos loaded into YouTube with the keyword "Egypt" for author, viewing, and creation date information.

We found four major types of content that typified Egyptian viral videos: raw protest and mobilization footage; citizen commentary; political punditry; and "soundtracks for the revolution." Raw protest and mobilization footage was the most common, totaling nearly 5.5 million views from 23 videos. One video featured a detailed 20-minute dialogue between a religious scholar and political philosopher about the future of Egypt, totaling 100,000 views. Another video featured a homemade video with a young girl's commentary about political events, totaling 275,000 views. But the most popular video, a music video, was heralded as a soundtrack to the revolution and served as a rallying cry of support for the Egyptian people's protests. This music video, uploaded on January 27, was the single most popular viral video for the Egyptian revolution, and it accounted for 25 percent of the top-20 video views.

## Gender Politics and the Politics of Inclusion

Digital information technologies mediate gender politics in unexpected ways. In the political economy of media, women are playing more dynamic roles in television and film both in front of and behind the camera. But women have, in the opinion of some observers, aggressively invaded the new public space created by digital media (Mernissi 2004). Marcotte, for example, has examined religious discourse regarding gender and sexuality, where forums have been essential spaces to challenge, contest, and even transgress traditional norms (Marcotte 2010). Some have even observed in very conservative societies and families, that Muslim women have begun to participate economically by running their own private online businesses (Ardalan 2002). First, digital media are allowing citizens to learn about the status of women and gender relations in other countries. Second, they also allow both men and women to debate specific gender issues relevant in their own cultures (Stowasser 2001). Third, the arrival of digital media in many Muslim communities and households has become an occasion for renegotiating and restructuring gender relationships. Finally, the internet supports women-only online communities, which have become sites for political conversation away from both patriarchal leaders and the public gaze of journalists. Political elites in some countries restrict internet access to prevent such cultural learning, discussion, and negotiation.

The introduction of new digital media does not simply provide the opportunity to redress gender disparities in developing communities; it is providing a platform for learning about gender politics. Three factors impede learning about gender politics in Muslim countries. First, new internet users rarely have the ability to conduct sophisticated searches and critically assess the content they find. This comes with practice, along with coaching from friends and family. Second, political elites in some countries actively work to discourage state programs from providing women with media training and access, or actively block listservs, blogs, and chat rooms where young Muslims can have some discourse on gender issues. Third, government regulators establish content filters that block websites they judge to be antithetical to the established edicts of gender relations in their country or according to their interpretation of Islam.

There is a growing literature about how exposure to digital media has an impact on users' levels of tolerance and empathy (Brundidge and Rice 2009; Robinson, Neustadtl, and Kestnbaum 2004). For many young Muslims, the online social networking applications and other content are the media by which they learn of life in other countries where faith and freedom can coexist. Networked information technologies are, at the very least, partly responsible for exposing citizens to liberal cultural values. Certainly some internet users in these countries can be radicalized through their internet use, but many will be sensitized through the internet. And in the case of Saudi Arabia, it may be the broadcast media on state-authorized channels that do more to reinforce conservative and Wahabbist interpretations of Islam. In Egypt, the broadcast media are certainly used to advance secularist perspectives of the role of faith in statecraft. One of the next steps in researching the impact of digital media in countries with large Muslim communities will be to investigate the overall impact of internet use on tolerance.

# Social Networking, Digital and Otherwise

For the most part, public opinion in countries with large Muslim communities has been a construction of ruling elites and state agencies. By so constraining the media diets of citizens, the ability of journalists to investigate popular sentiment, and the ability of researchers to survey the public, the boundaries of what constituted the "public" have been fundamentally constrained and knowledge of "opinion" deliberately kept vague. Today, political parties are using the internet to construct political opinion in a different way. By deeply integrating digital tools such as mobile phones and the internet into their systems of political communication, parties are able to reach and activate much larger numbers of people. In this way, the internet is actively used to challenge the basic relations of power because political parties use it to amass publics that were not previously reachable. Moreover, even where regimes allowed official opposition parties, the political actors who agreed to play by the rules of conduct had an easier time controlling broadcast media. Social networking applications have provided a new structure for the flow of political news and information, a structure that does not easily provide political elites with informational choke points. Without mandatory points of passage for political content and digital hosting services beyond the territorial control of these governments, social networking applications have had implications for who counts as the political public.

In countries where a handful of state agencies own the major media outlets, it is possible to define the public through the selection of topics covered in the news, through the framing of stories, and through the gender and ethnic representation of people who appear as journalists and as characters in news stories. It is rare, for example, to have immigrant Bengalis, Pakistanis, and Indians canvassed for opinion in the nightly newscasts in Saudi Arabia or the United Arab Emirates (UAE). Increasingly, the internet has become an alternative information source, one that holds content related to those minority voices.

But public opinion is not shaped by the internet in the sense that lots of citizens find interesting new public policy options online, but in the sense that these major media outlets have added the internet to their tool kit for measuring—and manipulating—public opinion. Media systems in these four countries were designed by the elites to make for easy manipulation by autocratic leaders or the Saudi royal family. Autocrats, by definition, work to constrain the size and diversity of their publics through media systems that distribute limited content to carefully defined groups. And it is the political parties, legal or not, that best use the internet to extend the definition of who the public is, by expanding their membership and increasing the rate of active contact. The social networking applications that facilitate the passage of political content over networks of family and friends provide not simply a competing media system but an alternative structure for distributing information.

## Conclusions

Social media played a crucial role in the political uprisings in Tunisia and Egypt. Using original data from multiple social media sources, we can offer some concrete conclusions about what that role was. First, social media played a central role in shaping political debates in the Arab spring. Second, a spike in online revolutionary conversations often preceded major events on the ground. Third, social media helped spread democratic ideas across international borders. But perhaps the most powerful evidence that digital media mattered in the Arab Spring comes from activists themselves.

Researchers with the *Arab Social Media Report* interviewed over a hundred protesters from both Tunisia and Egypt. In both countries, Facebook users were of the opinion that Facebook had been used primarily to raise awareness within their countries about the ongoing civil movements, spread information to the world about the movements, and organize activists and actions. Less than 15 percent in either country believed Facebook was primarily being used for entertainment or social reasons (Noman 2011). Surveys of participants in Tahrir Square demonstrations reveal that social media in general, and Facebook in particular, provided new sources of information the regime could not easily control and were crucial in shaping how citizens made individual decisions about participating in protests, the logistics of protest, and the likelihood of success. People learned about the protests primarily through interpersonal communication using Facebook, phone contact, or face-to-face conversation. Controlling for other factors, social media use greatly increased the odds that a respondent attended protests on the first day, and half of those surveyed produced and disseminated visuals from the demonstrations, mainly through Facebook (Tufekci and Wilson 2012).

Democratization movements existed in North Africa and the Middle East long before technologies such as mobile phones, the internet, and social media came to the region. However, with these technologies, people who share an interest in democracy learned to build extensive networks, create social capital, and organize political action. In both Tunisia and Egypt, these virtual networks materialized in the streets in early 2011 to help bring down two long-standing dictators.

Anecdotally, we know that social media played an important role at key moments in the events of 2011. But what are the big-picture trends in social media use that explain why public demand for democratic reform rose now and why events unfolded the way they did? The previous datasets reveal much about the role of different kinds of social media. The Tunisian blogosphere provided space for open political dialogue about regime corruption and the potential for political change. Twitter relayed stories of successful mobilization within and between countries. Facebook functioned as a central node in networks of political discontent in Egypt. During the protests, YouTube and other video archiving centers allowed citizen journalists, using mobile phone cameras and consumer electronics, to broadcast stories that the mainstream media could not or did not want to cover.

Social media alone did not cause political upheaval in North Africa. But information technologies—including mobile phones and the internet—altered the capacity of citizens and civil society actors to affect domestic politics. Social media have several kinds of impact on local systems of political communication. First, social media provide new opportunities and new tools for social movements to respond to conditions in their countries. It is clear that the ability to produce and consume political content, independent of social elites, is important because the public sense of shared grievances and potential for change can develop rapidly. Second, social media foster transnational links between individuals and groups. This means that network ties form between international and local democratization movements, and that compelling stories, told in short text messages or long-form video documentaries, circulate around the region. The inspiration of success in Tunisia was not just a fast-spreading contagion, for civil society leaders in neighboring countries also learned effective strategies of successful movement organizing through social media.

Social movements are traditionally defined as collective challenges, based on shared purposes, social solidarity, and sustained interactions with elites, opponents, and authorities. They support a public claim against target authorities and engage in political action by forming coalitions, organizing public meetings and demonstrations, and using the media to highlight their claims. Through such demonstrations and media use, social movements display their unity, numbers, and commitment. Social media, social networking applications, and consumer electronics have not changed the purpose of social movement organizing—economic opportunity and political voice are still the shared goals of social movements.

But in North Africa and the Middle East, relatively new youth movements have been surprised by the speed, size, and success of protests they have organized over social networking websites. Over several years they have found their political voice online and have held their meetings virtually. Each of the dictators in these countries has long had many political enemies, but they were a fragmented group of opponents. Now these opponents do more than use broadcast media to highlight their claims. They use social media to identify goals, build solidarity, and organize demonstrations. During the Arab Spring, individuals demonstrated their desire for freedom through social media, and social media became a critical part of the tool kit used to protest for freedom.

While several well-placed civic leaders and activists used digital media to organize political uprisings and communicate with the world, digital media were also used by regimes to respond to insurgencies. It would be a mistake to proceed without evaluating the ability of authoritarian regimes to use digital tools in their counterinsurgency strategy, so the next chapter evaluates the force of response—and degrees of success—that some governments had to the surge of popular protest for democracy.

# 4

# Authoritarian Responses and Consequences

Perhaps the best evidence that digital media were an important causal factor in the Arab Spring is that dictators treated them as such. The months during which the Arab Spring took place had the most national blackouts, network shutdowns, and tool blockages to date. But just as activists had a longer history of using digital media, authoritarian regimes had a history of responding to the political communication occurring over digital networks.

Long before the Arab Spring, on Friday, June 12, 2009, Iran voted, and when voters realized the election had been rigged, many poured into the streets in protest. Even then, social media websites such as Twitter and Facebook and SMS messaging were actively used to coordinate the movements of protesters and to get images and news out to the international community. Compared to protests that occurred the last time elections were stolen, the social movement lasted longer, drew in thousands more participants, and produced more witnesses to the brutal regime crackdown. Social media played a role in extending the life of civil disobedience. But while the theocratic regime did not fall, there were some important outcomes: the ruling mullahs were split in opinion about the severity of the crackdown. As part of the response, the regime attempted to disable national mobile phone networks. It disconnected the national internet information infrastructure for several hours and installed a deep packet inspection system that significantly slowed traffic. Until 2011, few regimes in North Africa and the Middle East had systematically disabled national information infrastructure in response to a political crisis.

Fast-forward six months to the early phase of the Arab Spring: the Tunisian and Egyptian regimes had notably different responses to the digital organization of protests. Long before the protests in December 2010 and January

2011, Tunisian officials had a long, repressive history of monitoring and targeting individuals engaging in online political activism. But during the protests, the government did not effectively control information networks to stop the outflow of local political conditions or the inflow of international reactions and support. Mobilized and well-informed, protesters benefited from the government's failure to manage sensitive information. Similarly, Egypt's Mubarak also failed to control information networks but in the end made a desperate attempt to shut down mobile networks. UK-based Vodafone complied with the Egyptian regime's demands to shut off mobile phones, which officials then used to send orders and misinformation to protesters. But these actions had the unintended consequence of increasing protest participation—organizer Waleed Rasheed said, "I would like to thank Mubarak so much . . . he disconnected mobile phones on January 27. More people came down to the streets on the 28th of January because he disconnected."

Yet authoritarian regimes have come to value digital media too. Security services in Bahrain, Iran, Saudi Arabia, and Syria observed how democracy advocates were using social media in Egypt and Tunisia, and they developed counterinsurgency strategies that allowed for surveilling, misleading, and entrapping protesters. New information technologies can be vital tools for social control (Aday et al. 2010; Howard 2010; Morozov 2011).

So it is not accurate to say that regimes are always disadvantaged by activists using digital technologies. While Tunisia and Egypt failed to act early and effectively to control digital networks, Libya and Bahrain did not. Turning off the internet was one of Gaddafi's first reactions. Before activists and citizens could learn about what was happening in neighboring cities, all outside news, as well as outcries for support from foreign diasporas, became effectively impossible to receive. In Bahrain, after failing to turn away protesters after many days of demonstrations, the regime responded by shutting off mobile networks early one morning. Shortly thereafter, the peaceful protesters were fired on with live ammunition. This occurred at a time when their ability to coordinate or to seek international support from foreign media was effectively blocked. In the days that followed, the government used the same social media sites protesters used to organize themselves by crowdsourcing the identifications of anonymous participants—or what Al Jazeera reporters have termed "a virtual lynch-mob."

Even Tunisian and Egyptian officials tried such surgical methods to punish dissenters. It is alleged that Tunisian authorities carried out "phishing" operations, to steal citizens' passwords to monitor and remove their content. Sofiene

Chourabi, a journalist and blogger, found himself unable to recover his email and Facebook accounts after they were hijacked. At the same time, content he had posted and pages he administered were deleted. "Here we don't really have internet, we have a national *intra-net*," said Azyz Amamy, a Tunisian web activist.

So what was the role of regimes in controlling information networks? How did their strategies impede the progress of digital activism, and under what circumstances did their efforts fail, backfire, or result in other unpredictable outcomes? How might understanding the strategies of repressive governments inform our understanding of the digital organization of social protest and political activism? For civil society actors around the world, digital media and online social networking applications have changed the way in which dissent is organized (Bimber, Flanagin, and Stohl 2005; Howard 2010; Still 2005). Social movement leaders from around the world use online applications and digital content systems to organize collective action, activate local protest networks, network with international social movements, and share their political perspective with global media systems (Byrne 2007; Kloet 2002; Shumate and Pike 2006).

In the past, authoritarian regimes easily controlled broadcast media in times of political crisis by destroying newsprint supplies, seizing radio and television stations, and blocking phone calls. It is certainly more difficult to control digital media on a regular basis, but there have been occasions when states have disabled a range of marginal to significant portions of their national information infrastructure. What situational tendencies cause state powers to specifically block internet access and disable digital networks? When do regimes resort to the more extreme measures of shutting off internet access? And when they do not have the capacity to control digital networks, how do states respond offline to dissent and criticism? What is the impact of doing so, and who is most affected?

Sophisticated repressive regimes often preemptively respond with a digital counterinsurgency strategy and often prepare for the day they need to battle their citizens either in the streets or in an information war. States such as China, Iran, and Saudi Arabia are excellent examples. China has invested a great deal of effort in constructing its virtual firewall, Iran has tested and implemented its own deep-packet inspection software purchased from Nokia, and Saudi Arabia has rerouted its internet cables through state-security servers in Riyadh to create a literal information bottleneck. Other countries, such as Egypt, Libya, and Yemen, did not have sophisticated long-term investments in managing information infrastructure. But when unexpected political turmoil arose, they developed responses that ranged from jailing and beating bloggers to more sophisticated strategies such as asking loyalists to identify protesters in photos posted on Facebook, creating domestic surveillance programs forcing citizens to monitor one another's activities, and more. In these instances, regimes used activists' spaces against them.

To conclude, we introduce examples and narratives along a spectrum of state sophistication with information technology, digital media censorship, the co-option of internet and mobile phone service providers, and the surveillance of civil society groups online. We look at the most intriguing examples of both clumsy and smart state responses. Egypt responded too late and with a strategy too unsophisticated to stop the information flow. Saudi Arabia and Syria responded very early and with very sophisticated offline and online strategies to curb the potential for protest mobilization. Technologies themselves do not possess liberatory potential—in important ways, authoritarian governments have actively learned new tricks from one another and from their mistakes.

## Decision Paths and Opportunity Structures

It is difficult to investigate patterns of state censorship. Many reports of censorship are essentially self-reported by technology users who assume there is a political reason behind their inability to connect to a digital network, whether mobile phone networks, gaming networks, or the internet. Sometimes the state admits to acts of censorship, which makes it easier to learn why the government has interfered and to what effect. At other times the state acts so clumsily or breaks the communication link between such large networks that many users can report being affected. While several researchers have studied the broad social impact of censorship, only a few have been able to provide evidence about both the shared perception that the state is surveilling its public and specific incidents of censorship that involve disconnections in digital networks (Deibert et al. 2008; Deibert et al. 2010). Drawing from multiple sources, however, it is possible to do a comparative analysis of the myriad of incidents in which government officials decide to censor their online publics.

The story of state censorship of information networks is not necessarily specific to non-democratic governments. And not all acts of state censorship are easy to describe and classify. One of the first incidents occurred on December

29, 1995, when German prosecutors demanded that an internet service provider (ISP) block 4 million worldwide subscribers from reading sex-related information on portions of the internet. This was the first instance of such drastic measures of state censorship, legislation, and regulation of information received online. Motivation for the shutdown came from a police investigation into child pornography in Bavaria, Germany. Though German officials were targeting 220,000 German subscribers when they asked for the block, CompuServe, the ISP in question, had no mechanism in place to limit just German users at the time and thus had to shut down service to all subscribers. In all, CompuServe restricted subscriber access to 200 newsgroups specifically related to the site Usenet. Reaction to the censorship elicited varied responses from community and civic groups. The National Center for Missing and Exploited Children, for example, hailed it as a form of "electronic citizenship." Meanwhile, groups such as the Electronic Frontier Foundation indicated concern and resistance to the notion of state control over individual rights online. The most current debate over internet censorship in a democratic country is taking place in Australia. Since 2008, the Australian Labor Party has pushed for a large-scale blocking of blacklisted foreign websites. If the measure passes, Australian internet service providers would be mandated to block such content, though the legislation to enact the censorship regulations has not yet been completed.

These early and recent incidents of state intervention with internet connectivity have brought forth questions that we still struggle to answer today: Who controls internet content? What are the legitimate reasons for state interference with digital networks? Over the last 15 years, states (both authoritarian and democratic) have become increasingly willing to interfere with the links between nodes of digital infrastructure. They do this by shutting out particular users or shutting off particular servers, by breaking the links to sub-networks of digital media, and sometimes even by disconnecting national information infrastructure from global networks. Recently, Research in Motion (RIM), the company behind the popular BlackBerry smartphone, has been involved in a complex issue involving several governments' requests to obtain better access to the server nodes in RIM's service networks. In the spring of 2010, a prominent political figure in the United Arab Emirates (UAE) used his BlackBerry's mobile camera to record himself torturing a Bangladeshi migrant worker. The video was taken and posted online, causing outrage from human rights groups and embarrassing the country's ruling elites. The UAE's response has been to demand that RIM provide dedicated servers within their territory so that the regime can monitor traffic and disable services as it chooses.

Eventually both Saudi Arabia and the United Arab Emirates threatened to ban the use of the popular BlackBerry smart phone. The UAE threatened to block access to text messages, email, and web browsers if RIM did not allow government access for security investigations. The threat of censorship could potentially affect more than half a million users of the most popular smartphone in the UAE. India followed suit, citing national security as the impetus for demanding that RIM stop encrypting data sent through their phones. Increasingly, private companies and ISP providers are being caught between meeting the security and information needs of their users and obeying imposed government regulations. Conceding, at least partially, to governmental pressure rather than risking a complete block, however, is more valuable to mobile and internet providers—BlackBerry, for example, is the most popular device connecting business elites and managers in these booming economies.

Since 1995—the year the National Science Foundation effectively privatized the internet (by decommissioning NSFNET and transitioning to several commercial networks)—there have been at least 526 occasions in which governments intervened in the connections of a digital network. Of these, about half were enacted by authoritarian regimes. The three countries with the highest number of incidents, China, Tunisia, and Turkey, represent both authoritarian and democratic regimes. In times of political uncertainty, rigged elections, or military incursions, ruling elites are sometimes willing to interfere with information infrastructure as a way of managing crises. In many of these cases, the targets (victims) are active domestic civil society movements with international linkages. When these movements organize, authoritarian governments can react harshly and invasively by blocking access to the global internet. Yet at the same time, these authoritarian regimes find that they cannot block internet access for extended periods, both because doing so has an impact on the national economy and because international political pressure becomes hard to ignore. During the heat of the protests in Tahrir Square, Mubarak demanded that the internet infrastructure be shut down; the loss to the national internet cost Egypt 4 percent of its annual GDP, or about $90 million dollars from a loss of revenue and global financial transactions. Similarly, on February 18, Libya abruptly turned off the entire internet before collapsing into civil war. Internet traffic fluctuations in Yemen also dropped briefly when the government was suspected of installing filtering software. Arbor Networks, an agency that monitors information security said, "We have never seen a country as connected as Egypt completely lose connectivity for such an extended period" (Labovitz 2011). Of 110 major internet providers worldwide during the Arab Spring protests, Bahrain and Libya had the most pronounced changes in internet traffic. Some blamed "overloaded circuits" while others suspected governments of enforced slowdowns of servers.

Shutting off the internet for a country's network also impacts the capacity of the state to respond to a crisis. Therefore, the decision tree for choking off internet access also involves some willingness to incapacitate portions of the government's security apparatus. Civil society groups do find methods to circumvent the blocked social media. A significant body of literature has grown around social movement use of newer digital media against authoritarian regimes (Garrett 2006; Marmura 2008a, b; McLaughlin 2003). While there is a healthy, ongoing conversation by scholars on the ways civil societies use digital media for social and political mobilization, studies are rare that examine the motivations, tactics, and impacts of government responses to online civic activity.

Comparative case analyses of the occasions in which regimes disconnected significant portions of their national digital infrastructure, including mobile phones and internet access, can help illuminate this issue. We need to define the range of situations in which states have actually disrupted large sections of their own national information infrastructure, evaluate the outcomes for regime stability and civil society, and advance collective action theory through a typology of regime-based censorship of digital hardware and digital content. Through this typology we argue for the importance of the regime in shaping the political economy of ICT infrastructures. After all, activists must operate within the overall information infrastructure available to them in the market, which the government has a heavy hand in shaping. While some have argued that the state no longer has strong control of media production and consumption systems, there are many occasions when a state can exercise power over digital networks.

## How Do States Interfere with Digital Networks?

The internet has become an invaluable logistical tool for organization and communication among civil society groups. It is an information infrastructure mostly independent of the state, and since civil society groups are by definition social organizations independent of the state, the internet has become an important incubator for social movements and civic action. Some governments work hard to censor digital media, but even in such countries the internet is difficult to control. Governments might own nodes in the network, but rarely can they completely choke off network connections. This means that tools such as You-Tube, Twitter, Facebook, and email are useful, and at sensitive times, critical organizational tools. In some of the toughest authoritarian regimes, these tools are crucial because face-to-face conversations about political life are so problematic. For civil society groups these tools are often content distribution systems largely independent of the state. But there are numerous circumstances in which governments and repressive regimes have learned to co-opt or limit these opportunities for autonomous civic action. The internet has altered the dynamics of political communication systems in many countries, such that the internet itself is the site of political contestation between the state and civil society.

States interfere with digital networks using many tactics with various levels of severity. Generally, all states, including democracies, emerging democracies, authoritarian regimes, and fragile states, have targeted members of civil society. They have done so online by shutting down websites or portals; offline by arresting journalists, bloggers, activists, and citizens; by proxy through controlling internet service providers, forcing companies to shut down specific websites, or denying access to content the state considers disagreeable; and, in the most extreme cases, shutting down access to entire online and mobile networks. Surprisingly, while authoritarian regimes generally attempt to control full networks, sub-networks, and nodes more than democracies do, democracies are more likely to target civil society actors by proxy through control of internet service providers. Table 4.1 presents cases where governments exercised control by targeting full networks (shutting down the internet), sub-networks (blocking websites), and network nodes (targeting individuals), and by proxy (pressuring service providers).

Event-history analysis is a commonly used comparative method for examining the real circumstances of political crises. More important, it is particularly useful for developing a nuanced understanding of relatively new social phenomena and for building typologies and categories of political action. Drawing on a range of sources, we built a unique collection of detailed event logs for major disruptions in digital networks of nations between 1995 and 2011. We collected information about incidents as reported in major news media, specialized news sources such as national security and information security blogs, and other online forums for discussing such topics.

A case is defined as an occasion when a government intervened in a digital network by breaking or turning off connections between national sub-networks

*Table 4.1* **How Do States Disconnect Their Digital Networks? Incidents by Regime Type**

|  | Democracy | Emerging Democracy | Authoritarian | Fragile | Total |
|---|---|---|---|---|---|
| Complete Network Shutdown (Full Networks) | 13 | 3 | 30 | 3 | 49 |
| Specific Site-oriented Shutdowns (Sub-Networks) | 140 | 25 | 210 | 8 | 383 |
| Individual Users (Nodes) | 82 | 16 | 125 | 3 | 226 |
| By Proxy Through ISP | 47 | 4 | 41 | 4 | 96 |

*Source*: Based on authors' calculations, replication data available at www.pitpi.org.

and global information networks. Sometimes this meant blocking ports or access to a particular sub-network of digital media, such as content at the domains Facebook or YouTube. In times of significant political or military crisis, such as war or contested elections, the governments might disconnect SMS messaging services or block the entire country's access to global networks. Additionally, regimes may target individual actors in networks. But these incidents are more than general government threats of surveillance or intimidation (which are also forms of censorship). They are distinct incidents when government officials made the specific decision to disable the links or nodes in the portions of the information networks they can control.

Since the literature on digital censorship often makes a distinction between democracies, emerging democracies, and authoritarian regimes, we rely on the Polity IV data about regime type (Marshall and Jaggers 2010). In addition, since several of the governments appearing in the event log are too fragile to be placed definitively into one of these three categories, we rely on Polity IV data for a category of fragile regimes. As per Polity IV coding, if a state was recovering from civil war or foreign military invasion, experiencing a complex humanitarian disaster, or had effectively failed for other reasons, we coded this state as fragile. A state's regime type was set according to the Polity IV score for that state in the year of the reported incident. Several countries had several incidents, and it is possible that regime types changed over time.

In all, there were 566 unique incidents involving 101 countries: 39 percent of the incidents occurred in democracies, 7 percent in emerging democracies, 51 percent in authoritarian regimes, and 2 percent in fragile states. Each incident was coded for the name of the country in which a state agency intervened in digital networks, the year of the incident, the type of regime, and a precise date if available. We made general notes on the narrative of each incident and mapped on the Polity IV score for the country in the year of the incident. Then we developed three standardized typologies for the kinds of incidents being reported. First, we developed a category that iteratively helped define the case and a typology of actions that states take against social media. Second, we developed a category for the reason a state took that action, sometimes relying on third-party reports if the state simply denied any interference. Finally, we developed a category for the impact of the interference.

While we might expect authoritarian regimes to interfere more aggressively with their digital infrastructure than other types of regimes, Figure 4.1 reveals that democracies also substantively disconnect their communication networks—with at least 80 incidents a year occurring in recent years. Only a fraction of these involve emerging democracies, but Figure 4.1 provokes more questions. Over time, it appears that all types of regimes have become

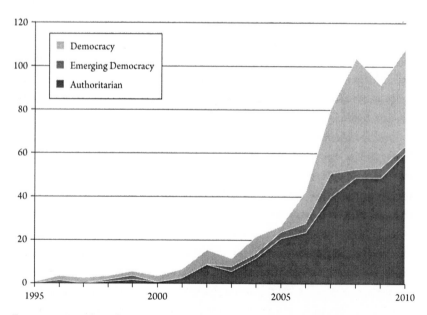

*Figure 4.1* Number of Major Incidents of State Intervention in Digital Networks, by Regime Type, 1995–2011.

*Note*: In total, there were 566 incidents before April 2011. Regime type is tied to the specific year in which the incident was recorded.

more and more willing to interfere with information access. As social media have diffused, they have become a fundamental infrastructure for collective action. Even though democracies appear just as aggressive as authoritarian regimes in disconnecting digital networks, are there differences in the ways such states intervene? What are the different reasons for such drastic interventions (see Table 4.2)?

The most extreme form of network control occurs when states shut down access to the internet entirely. Authoritarian regimes have done so significantly more than fragile states and emerging democracies, and also twice as often as democracies. For example, China shut down internet services in the Xinjiang region after ethnic riots erupted in 2006. The riots resulted in 140 fatalities, and the state has since blocked access to Twitter and other social networking sites to control the conflict and dissent. Pakistan also severely restricted the internet after a US-based cartoonist organized the "Everybody Draw Mohammed Day." After the event attracted 43,000 fans from around the world, the Pakistani government began banning content. Emerging democracies such as Haiti and Thailand have engaged in shutting down internet service providers and entire online networks like YouTube. Thousands of Haitians lost internet access in 1999 when the government allegedly attempted to silence dissent and consolidate power under the guise of punishing Alpha Network Communications for selling telephone cards and providing international telephone services. Bangladesh blocked YouTube and most other file-sharing services after recordings of a meeting between the prime minister and senior army officers were leaked. Thailand, also an emerging democracy with a record of political online censorship, maintains a block on entire internet services like YouTube. Guatemala, a democracy, also blocked entire networks when a political crisis over the murder of a prominent lawyer raged on the WordPress network. These examples suggest that although complete network shutdowns are least common, they tend to materialize when states face national controversies and moments of severe social and political unrest, often (but by no means exclusively) in authoritarian regimes.

These examples and narratives surrounding the circumstances when governments are most likely to limit or shut off internet and mobile services were replayed during the Arab Spring. But the Arab Spring also led to some important innovations and advancements in states' strategies for managing information networks, either as long-term investments or more sophisticated short-term responses. For example, the US Department of State has commented that many Arab regimes engaged in second- and

*Table 4.2.* **Why Do States Disconnect Their Digital Networks? Incidents by Regime Type**

| | Democracy | Emerging Democracy | Authoritarian | Fragile | Total |
|---|---|---|---|---|---|
| *Protecting Authority* | | | | | |
| Protecting Political Leaders and State Institutions | 30 | 7 | 23 | 1 | 61 |
| Election Crisis | 4 | 3 | 9 | 0 | 16 |
| Eliminating Propaganda | 5 | 1 | 24 | 0 | 30 |
| Mitigating Dissidence | 8 | 5 | 11 | 3 | 27 |
| National Security | 29 | 6 | 34 | 0 | 69 |
| *Preserving the Public Good* | | | | | |
| Preserving Cultural and Religious Morals | 27 | 4 | 37 | 6 | 74 |
| Preserving Racial Harmony | 9 | 0 | 1 | 0 | 10 |
| Protecting Children | 30 | 0 | 2 | 0 | 32 |
| Cultural Preservation | 2 | 0 | 19 | 0 | 21 |
| Protecting Individual's Privacy | 3 | 0 | 2 | 0 | 5 |
| Dissuading Criminal Activity | 29 | 3 | 18 | 1 | 51 |
| Alleged System Failure, Neither Denied Nor Admitted | 4 | 4 | 9 | 0 | 17 |
| Censorship Denied By State | 3 | 1 | 11 | 0 | 15 |
| Unknown, Other | 40 | 4 | 90 | 4 | 138 |
| Total | 223 | 38 | 290 | 15 | 566 |

*Source*: Based on authors' calculations, replication data available at www.pitpi.org.

third-generation strategies (Marks 2011). First-generation strategies were limited to buying online censorship software from Silicon Valley and installing it in-country. Second- and third-generation strategies are more sophisticated and effective. For example, governments have organized "denial-of-service" attacks on human rights or activist organizations' websites: flooding their sites with so many requests that it effectively crashes organizational servers and prevents other citizens from accessing their content. Some regimes sent malware and viruses to websites to infect programming and hardware. Although second- and third-generation strategies are more effective, the ultimate strategy used by many regimes in the Arab Spring was to completely turn off access.

Unlike the most extreme measure of shutting down entire online networks, states are most likely to target individual websites (online) or their producers and users (offline). Democracies are much more likely to engage in online content censorship than other tactics, though they also frequently target civil society members offline. The earliest case of a democracy shutting down online sub-networks was the aforementioned German attempt in 1995. In 1996, German authorities again removed access to banned material, including a Dutch online magazine. More recently, Australia, as of July 2010, is considering a mandatory internet filter to censor a list of URLs associated with child sexual abuse, bestiality, sexual violence, crime, violence, drug use, and content advocating violence and extremism.

While socially questionable material and content promoting criminal activities are commonly cited reasons for blocking online material in democratic states, some states have used the same tactic for dealing with foreign policy disputes. In August 2010, South Korea engaged in an online dispute with North Korea over social media when South Korean citizens were threatened by the South Korean government with arrest for accessing North Korea's Twitter feed. However, despite attempting to reroute requests from North Korea's Twitter page to a warning page, North Korea's page accumulated more than 9,000 followers. In instances like this, when states are unable to block online content effectively, they are forced to move more directly toward censoring individuals. Authoritarian states do this most often, and in many cases, with more severity. Bloggers, journalists, and social activists are the most common individual targets of offline censorship, often facing arrest and fines. Following Thailand's military coup in 2006, two cyber dissidents were arrested for comments made about the monarchy in online discussion boards, and they now face a minimum sentence of 15 years in prison. Another example of online activities leading to offline government reactions is Cuba's arrests of two online journalists working for CubaNet in 2005 and 2007. These journalists were arrested for engaging in "subversive propaganda" and "precriminal social danger."

While democracies engage in censoring individual users, like authoritarian regimes, they also have a unique tendency to target individuals providing the infrastructure. In fact, democracies have a slightly higher rate of blocking content and controlling civil actors through indirect measures, such as targeting internet service providers. Turkey and Italy, both democracies, have legally pursued charges against both internet service providers and their users. In March 2010, an Italian court convicted three Google executives for not removing violent video content that appeared on their online services. In August 2009, Malawi approved legal measures to pressure internet service providers to monitor social networking sites such as Twitter and Facebook. Hungary and Belgium have also shared experiences where internet service providers have come under pressure to approve "notices of takedown" procedures from their governments, a process whereby online hosts remove content in response to court orders or allegations of copyright infringement. This could be because much of the global information infrastructure is based out of advanced economies, such as the United States, Germany, the United Kingdom, and France. Authoritarian regimes often do not have direct control over these foreign entities, other than through state-run ISPs based in Tripoli, Riyadh, Cairo, and other countries. Surprisingly, while authoritarian regimes are more likely to fine and imprison civil society actors directly for criticizing the regime and its elites, democracies have more examples of regimes using legal frameworks and roundabout measures for targeting both internet service providers and their users.

## Why Do States Interfere with Digital Networks?

Governments interfering with digital networks often justify their actions by saying they are merely protecting public officials and state institutions, or preserving the "public good." Authoritarian regimes often do so during election crises, to eliminate propaganda and mitigate dissidence in the purported interest of national security. Public officials cite "terrorism threats" and preventing the spread of "state secrets" as reasons to do so. For example, the Bahraini government turned the state media against protesters, broadcasting messages encouraging citizens to report the identities of Shia dissidents inciting criticism against the Sunni government. Undermining authority figures is a frequent reason for justifying digital interference by non-democratic regimes. As far back as 2007, Kazakh officials shut down opposition websites because of published transcripts and recordings related to a public battle between authoritarian President Nursultan Nazarbayev and his estranged son-in-law.

Because sensitive communications such as these can be used by dissident groups for propaganda purposes, governments also target online activists legally as well. In 2003, China sentenced a user to four years in prison for discussing and posting information about democracy over email, online forums, and chat rooms. Established democracies such as the United States have also attempted to discourage dissidence. In 2009, two citizens were arrested for tweeting about police locations during G20 protests in Pittsburgh, Pennsylvania. Although regimes interfere with digital networks to preserve regime legitimacy, election periods are especially sensitive times for authoritarian regimes. These elections, although often forged and rigged, present a lucrative opportunity for pro-democracy activists to illuminate the public about government corruption. Regimes are on higher alert during these periods to intervene and eliminate conversations about corruption prior to, during, or after elections. During the contentious Iranian elections of 2009, officials first slowed and then shut down access to the entire Twitter network, heavily used by protest movements to coordinate and share information about the contested elections. Similarly, Egyptian citizens have been known to post footage of votes being counted, with clear evidence of forgery and bribing, on YouTube. While the Iranian regime was very sophisticated in tracking, deleting, and arresting these activists, Egyptian state security was not.

While authoritarian regimes (and sometimes established democracies) will justify digital interventions as a means to protect public officials and state institutions, they must also engage in some rhetorical gymnastics to justify their actions as being in the interest of the public good. States also disable social media by claiming an urgent need to preserve the public good and, sometimes, public safety. During the Arab Spring, preserving cultural and religious morals (Saudi Arabia), preserving racial harmony (Bahrain), and dissuading criminal activity (Egypt) were common reasons cited for shutting off social media and mobile networks.

Officials attribute intervention to preventing the spread of blasphemous or offensive information that challenges the religious and cultural morality of the state. This is especially true of Saudi Arabia and other Islamist regimes. A comprehensive project by the Open-Net Initiative investigating religiously sanctioned censorship found that "religion-based internet censorship bars the free flow of information in many majority Muslim countries by means of regulatory restrictions and ISP-level technical filtering that blocks objectionable web content. When regimes implement and enforce faith-based censorship they create borders around certain content. . . . For example, many majority Muslim countries criminalize the promotion of non-Islamic faiths among their Muslim citizens offline" (Noman 2011). Because many authoritarian regimes in the Arab world maintain legitimacy by relying on religious sanction, censoring religious content and perspectives is as critical as censoring other types of political information (Noman 2011).

The long list of countries that engage in religiously sanctioned censorship of sensitive political information include Bahrain, Gaza, Kuwait, Morocco, Oman, Qatar, Saudi Arabia, Sudan, Tunisia, the UAE, and Yemen. These cases involve targeting websites and individuals who access or distribute "anti-Islamic" (a category frequently used to block anything threatening to the regime or local power elites) or pornographic material. For example, Pakistan blocked access to 450 sites in 2009, including Facebook and YouTube, after an international event to depict the Prophet Mohammed was organized on Facebook. In another example, Iran shut down access to YouTube and Amazon, in 2006, to "purge the country of Western influence."

Regimes sometimes justify their actions by claiming to protect public safety. Reducing criminal acts is used as a reason to justify interventions when individuals have been arrested for copyright infringement, distribution of illegal information, and participation in activities deemed illegal by the state. Individuals have often been prosecuted for breaking the law in their home countries. For example, in 2009, Polish authorities arrested the creators of a peer-to-peer portal and shut down the site because of alleged copyright infringement. On the other hand, long before the Arab Spring, Tunisian citizens were fined and jailed for "causing harm by means of telecommunication networks" when they filmed and posted content online without an official permit or written consent of those being filmed.

## Conclusion: The Causes and Consequences of Digital Interventions

The lasting impact of a temporary disconnection in internet service may actually be a strengthening of weak ties between global and local civil society networks. When civil society disappears from the grid, others notice. What lasts are the ties between a nation's civic groups, and between international non-governmental organizations and like-minded, in-country organizations. Certainly not all of these virtual communities are about elections, but their existence is a political phenomenon particularly in countries where state and social elites have worked hard to police offline communities. Thus, even the bulletin boards and chat rooms dedicated to shopping for brand-name watches are sites that practice free speech and where the defense of free speech is a topic of conversation. The internet allows opposition movements that are based outside of a country to reach in and become part of the system of political communication within even the strictest authoritarian regimes. Today, banning political parties could simply mean that formal political opposition will move to organize online, from outside the country. It also means that civil society leaders may turn to other organizational forms permitted by network technologies.

When states disconnect particular social media services, student and civil society leaders develop creative workarounds and relearn traditional (offline) mobilization tactics. This almost always means that target sites, such as YouTube, Facebook, and Twitter, are accessible through other means. When regimes cannot successfully shut off online dissidence and autonomous civil conversations, they are forced to look outward. Sometimes, it is possible to have enough leverage through international relations or legal frameworks to successfully curb an opposition movement. In March 2011, a Facebook page supporting the Palestinian intifada was pulled down by Facebook after the Israeli government complained that the page was inciting violence against Jews. In authoritarian regimes, such as Saudi Arabia, the UAE, Bahrain, and others, such an act is not as easy. These regimes must work hard to curb online dissidence internally in creative ways. When 40 Saudi women staged a rare demonstration in Riyadh demanding the release of prisoners held without trial, they were supported by an online campaign calling for political reform and launched on Facebook. In April 2011, prominent blogger and democratic activist Ahmed Mansoor was conveniently charged with possession of alcohol and arrested (after receiving death threats online). He had been petitioning for political representation and legislative powers for democratic institutions.

Beyond arrests and beatings, government responses have become more sophisticated. In the case of Mansoor, a Facebook page called "Ahmed Mansoor, a traitor without a nation" was created to defame the activist and his work. These tactics have been echoed in neighboring countries as well.

Bahraini officials responded to Shia activists by not only firing on peaceful protesters but also creating what Al Jazeera English has called "a virtual lynch mob." The Facebook pages used by Bahraini activists were turned against them to hunt down organizers and participants through crowd-sourced identification of individuals in online photographs and videos. Once identified, many of these citizens were arrested, publicly defamed online and on state media, and tortured, and some killed, by Bahraini authorities.

When a political, military, or other security crisis is over, what remains is the lasting impact of a temporary outage in digital network connectivity. The internet has become a crucial component of political communication during elections—even rigged ones. It has also become a crucial component of political communication during other kinds of regime transition, such as executive turnover, foreign military intervention, natural disasters, and social protests that challenge in a very fundamental way a regime's legitimacy. Information infrastructure is not simply part of the general context of contemporary social mobilization. Indeed, social computing is a defining feature of elections. Digital media such as mobile phones and the internet now help incubate civic conversations, especially in countries that heavily censor the national print and broadcast media.

Internet access is often limited to wealthy social elites, but these elites have a key role in either accepting or rejecting the outcome of an election. The internet has become a necessary infrastructure for the development of civil society, and election season is often the time for civic groups to be most active. Most, though not all, of the regimes studied in this event catalogue are authoritarian, or were when the decision to disconnect from global information networks was taken. For authoritarian regimes, the single greatest threat to stability is often internal elite defection. When a cohort of wealthy families, educated and urban elites, and government employees decide they no longer wish to back a regime, it is likely to fail. In most of the countries studied here, only a small fraction of the population has internet access through computers and mobile phones. However, this small population is the one for which authoritarian regimes work hard to broker information.

It is not Twitter, blogs, or YouTube that cause social unrest. But today, successful social movement organizing and civic engagement is difficult to imagine without this suite of social media tools, even in countries such as Iran, Egypt, or Tunisia. Many people in these countries have no internet or mobile-phone access. Nevertheless, the people who do—urban dwellers, educated elites, and the young—are precisely the population with the capacity to enable regime change or to tacitly support electoral outcomes. These are the populations who support or defect from authoritarian rule, and for whom connections to family and friends have demonstrably changed with technology diffusion. Comparative analysis reveals the degree to which different regimes feel threatened by social media, whether such tools are actively used to organize dissent, or passively used for producing and consuming culture.

When digital networks are reactivated, personal networks that cross international boundaries also reactivate. Digital outages have become sensitive moments in which student leaders, journalists, and civil society groups experiment with digital technologies. Even if their favorite candidates are not elected, the process of experimentation with digital media is important because it infuses more information habits and news diets independent of the state into their daily engagement with public life.

Information infrastructure *is* politics. And the political culture that we now see online during elections comes not just from political elites but also from citizens: using social media, documenting human rights abuses with their mobile phones, sharing spreadsheets to track state expenditures, and pooling information about official corruption. Perhaps the most lasting impact of digital media use during crises is that people get accustomed to being able to consume *and* produce political content. When regimes disconnect from global information infrastructures, they employ a range of stop-gap measures that usually reinforce public expectation for global connectivity. One of the things authoritarian regimes did consistently during the Arab Spring was to block citizens from reading international news and activists from reaching international journalists. On the eve of major protests in Tahrir Square, one protestor noted, "If Al Jazeera turns off its cameras tonight, there will be a massacre in Tahrir Square." In the following chapter we explore why activists, even primarily digital activists, rely so heavily on international news organizations, but also why non-democratic regimes loathe them so much.

# 5

## Al Jazeera, Social Media, and Digital Journalism

This is why I no longer have the control over the country
that I once had.
—*Mubarak to diplomat in-flight over Cairo, pointing to the
forest of television antennas below, 1995*

If you switch off your cameras tonight, there will be
genocide. . . . You are protecting us by showing what is
happening in Tahrir Square.
—*Caller from Tahrir Square to director of Al Jazeera
network, January 25, 2011*

Yes, we may have helped Tunisia, Egypt. But let us not
forget the elephant in the room: Al Jazeera + sat dishes.
—*WikiLeaks' tweet, January 29, 2011*

In previous chapters, we demonstrated the ways in which social media provided new capacities and constraints on a range of political actors, from desperate democracy activists to traditional political parties and tough dictators. But we would be remiss not to look into the important changes in how journalists work and to the role of news organizations since news consumers in the region began using technologies like mobile phones and the internet to read and produce news. In many of the countries caught up in revolutionary fervor, it was a small group of civic leaders who first used digital media in creative ways to reach a wider public eager for political change. But in recent years, an even wider public began using consumer electronics in ways that changed the dynamics of news markets. And as a news agency, Al Jazeera has been the most adept and autonomous at keeping up with media habits and demands of people in the region.

Across North Africa and the Middle East, a growing cohort of citizens now consumes more international news than ever before. There is some evidence that the news sources are primarily Al Jazeera, the BBC, CNN, and other international news organizations with a vivid online presence. This is an important development because regimes that used to be able to play distinct domestic and international political games through state-owned media can no longer do so to the same degree. Distinctions between local and international news are intertwined for many citizens. During the Arab Spring protests, Arab citizens learned about what was happening in Amman and compared it with what took place in neighboring Cairo, as well as in international Western hubs with large overseas diasporas such as Paris, Toronto, and Chicago. How did news of their experiences reach regional and international readers so quickly and efficiently? What role did the mainstream news organizations play in this critical diffusion of information? And how are traditional broadcast networks forging new ways of operating in environments where activists can effectively operate side by side?

In this chapter we discuss the indispensable role broadcast organizations, such as Al Jazeera English, played in amplifying social media narratives internationally. Al Jazeera is a fascinating case study in how traditional news media helped create new linkages among civil society actors within and between countries. Unlike many Western news cultures that socialize journalists to maintain a healthy distance from the subjects of their coverage, news cultures in North Africa and the Middle East operate more nimbly and cooperate with citizen journalists. Embedded in digital environments, participatory citizen bloggers upload user-generated content through mobile phones, and activists reach out directly to journalists. Newly established news organizations such as Al Jazeera English played a critical role operating not only alongside digital activists, but acting hand-in-hand with them.

During the height of the protests in Tahrir Square, activists pleaded with Al Jazeera to not stop filming, saying, "If you switch off your cameras tonight, there will be genocide.... You are protecting us by showing what is happening in Tahrir Square" (Bosker 2011). In notable contrast were Libya and Bahrain, where broadcast journalists were not present and protest movements were notably less successful and more violent. First, we treat Al Jazeera as a news organization and discuss the role of digital media in shaping organizational and product innovation. Then we discuss the impact of media privatization on the political economy of news in the region and the growing market for news about local events among each country's global diaspora. Subsequently, we make the argument that in the absence of legitimate opportunities to be a citizen through voting and public assembly, generating content for blogs and news sites has become, in recent years, one form of civic expression for people in several countries across the region. Citizen journalists have been carrying out some of the most vociferous critiques, and the habits of citizen journalism spread widely in the moments of crisis in early 2011.

## Al Jazeera, Digital Media, and the Changing Organization of News

The online and broadcast audience for Al Jazeera's news products has grown over the years, though it certainly varies from country to country. But during the Arab Spring, Al Jazeera was instrumental in constructing a news audience in two ways. First, it covered stories that the national news media in many countries would not, particularly at times when citizens wanted those stories. Second, as an independent organization it remained active and "live" as a news agency when governments shut down domestic news agencies. Third, Al Jazeera actively cultivated content from citizens, providing fresh, local content that news consumers wanted.

Al Jazeera is probably the most widely read single online news source in the Arab world. Its content is frequently updated and is thematically consistent across English and Arabic versions (Abdul-Mageed 2008). Yet, compared to Western media, there are definite differences in the frames used. Websites for the *New York Times* and the *Guardian* consistently framed the Iraq war as a project in rebuilding the country. In contrast, Al Jazeera and *Al Ahram*—the newspaper of record for the Egyptian government—framed the Iraq war in terms of conflict and strife using negative tones and terms (Dimitrova and Connolly-Ahern 2007). Online news sources still exhibit cultural biases: news sources from the United States and countries in the "Coalition of the Willing" produced positive content, human-interest stories, and media self-coverage; news sources in Egypt, Malaysia, Pakistan, Turkey, and the UAE framed the war in terms of responsibility (Dimitrova et al. 2005). For many Arab citizens, online news sites are not just an alternative to state-run or state-censored sources but are an alternative to Western news sources. Regular Arab readers find Al Jazeera online more respectful of religion, culture, and tradition than the CNN and BBC websites (Barkho 2006).

In important ways, digital technologies allow citizens to surveil the activities of their states. During Israel's invasion of Gaza in December 2008, Al Jazeera developed an application for collecting incident reports from the ground using SMS technology and Twitter (Al Jazeera English 2009). As Anderson and Eickelman conclude, online Arab newspapers "collectively constitute a new community of communication that is transnational, open to more participants, and interactive in a way that traditional broadcasting has not been" (Eickelman and Anderson 2003). For example, analysis of articles published during the second Iraq War on Al Arabiya's site and reader responses to those articles reveal that that Arab readers not only challenged the views of Al Arabiya about the war, but they also offered their own versions of events (Al-Saggaf 2004). Moreover, in their responses, readers also posted news about the events covered that they obtained from other satellite television stations, such as Al Jazeera or from websites in which news was reported by people who witnessed or were involved in the events themselves (Al-Saggaf 2006).

Online journalism is subject to many of the constraints and pressures that can beleaguer the production of news in print or for broadcast. Sensational stories are given the most hype, broadcast time, or screen space. Research on Al Jazeera's site has consistently revealed that military and political violence, politics, and foreign relations are priorities for its editors, and these stories in turn receive the most commentary from its online readership. The capacity for debate has grown significantly in the vast majority of Muslim communities around the developing world. Historically, the capacity for debate over Islamic texts has expanded whenever new information technologies have been introduced (Miller 2007; Rao 2003). More recently, Al Jazeera helped satisfy a hunger for debate in the Arab world by covering Arab issues in depth and hosting debates from a diversity of perspectives: from feminists and traditionalists, Arab nationalists and non-Arab separatists, mullahs and secular parliamentarians, apostate scholars, and authoritarian apologists (Ghareeb 2000).

## Media Privatization and the Political Economy of News

When Bouazizi set himself on fire on December 17, Tunisia's state-run media did not cover the incident. Indeed, the first state coverage appeared two weeks later, when Ben Ali deigned to visit Bouazizi in the hospital. In the intervening period, citizens turned the plight of a disaffected shopkeeper *into* news. Ben

Ali went to the hospital not because of mainstream media pressured him to do so but because Tunisians had created a news event through online social networks without the help of state media; Ben Ali had to respond. These citizen journalists were able to operate because of the proliferation of internet access and sophisticated, digitally mediated civic innovations that have taken root over the last five years. To unpack how broadcast media and social media networks have hybridized, we must refer to examples from before the Arab Spring as well as during the protest period. In Morocco, when 37,000 protesters poured out onto the streets on February 20, human rights groups and labor unions were not the only ones responsible for organizing them—journalists were also critical to the mass mobilizations and joined in. The Overseas Press Club of America reports that more than 450 journalists were attacked throughout the Arab Spring movements. Ironically, it is perhaps WikiLeaks' January 29 post on Twitter that most accurately describes the importance of news organizations in the Arab Spring: "Yes, we may have helped Tunisia, Egypt. But let us not forget the elephant in the room: Al Jazeera + sat dishes."

Because much of the North African and Middle Eastern societies have not enjoyed the right to free political discourse through uncensored public information systems, Arab public opinion has been simplistically assumed to be monolithic and cynical. State censorship of public discourse has also been credited with the seclusion of political discussion to private spheres, with few opportunities for public deliberation. However, the events of the Arab Spring present important contradictions to traditional understandings of public opinion formation in North Africa and the Middle East. First, digital media have provided many new spaces for free and semi-public political discussion. Second, much of this space takes on an element of transnational and transregional (Zayani 2008) engagement across diverse Arab and Western audiences—both local audiences and diasporas seem to be enjoying access to the same types of political information. This shared discourse allows for learning about shared grievances across borders, and especially by overseas diasporas.

Khamis offers a two-part explanation for the contemporary development of Arab media ecology: the state-dominated broadcast era and the post-broadcast digital era (Khamis 2011). Before the 1990s, media ownership in many Arab states was largely dominated by governments under strict political censorship norms. In this era, Arab citizens found it difficult to learn about political events and engage in political discussion. Also in this era, print media enjoyed some political liberty to test the boundaries of state-monitored status quos because readership was limited to the highly literate and political elites of societies. On the other hand, broadcast media did not share this political liberty; media ownership before the 1990s was mainly locally based, and top-down organizational hierarchies made it easy for non-democratic governments to coerce journalists to play by party rules. During and after the 1990s, however, many important economic and legal changes took place across Arab media systems.

First, media privatization, like that in Egypt, led to direct broadcast satellite television being introduced in the region. Laws that carefully monitored news workers were also altered in a struggle to keep up. For example, many of Egypt's press laws were removed in 2006, while media rights and journalism advocacy organizations funded by media-development programs began to thrive (Hamdy 2009). Similarly, Morocco, which until 2006 had only two radio and two television stations, established more private radio and television stations—all while regulatory codes struggled to keep up with the changing media environment (Hidass 2010). Second, large-scale foreign military interventions like the First Gulf War paved the way for non-Arab news organizations to acquire firsthand footage, such as CNN's introduction to the region. Previously isolated Arab publics began having direct exposure to international images and events. Consequently, Arab regimes and their state-run television channels lost a significant monopoly on official versions of the public narrative. Third, media privatization and the introduction of non-Arab news outfits also coincided with the diffusion of internet access to private citizens. Tunisians were the first to gain internet access (1991), followed by Egyptians, Algerians, the citizens of the Emirates, and then Kuwaitis (1993), then Jordanians, Bahrainis, Lebanese, and Moroccans (1994–5), and last, Yemenis, Omanis, Saudis, and Syrians (1996–7)(Oghia and Indelicato 2011).

Since the ushering in of the post-broadcast digital era, online civil society has flourished in the Arab world, with popular social media destinations such as Facebook skyrocketing (Mourtada and Salem 2011); 2 million Algerians, 6.5 million Egyptians, 1.4 million Jordanians, 1 million Lebanese, 3.2 million Moroccans, 4 million Saudis, 2.3 million Tunisians, and 2.4 million Emiratis use social media regularly to access international news information. For this growing membership of online civil society, access to a diverse array of political information was not only possible but it was also a crucial new opportunity to seed autonomous political engagement. New satellite stations and print newspapers hosted themselves online with the growth of internet accessibility, making it easier for more uncensored sources of international news information. Faced with an increasingly young and college-educated labor pool, government efforts to join information society development initiatives necessitated Arab regimes' compliance with access to information laws and instrumental openness on the web. For example, the UAE does not have such laws but is ranked as #12 by the United Nations on e-government measures (Relly and Cuillier 2010). Similarly, Jordan has taken a lead in making information society building a national priority—such as improving e-government services, facilitating the growth of the private information technology sector, and generally improving quality of public life (Nagi and Hamdan 2009).

Between the late 1980s and now, the era of monolithic state-controlled and government-owned media environments in many Middle Eastern nations has shifted to a more privatized and non-hierarchically organized digital public information infrastructure for their citizens. These shifts mostly began after the 1990s and have accelerated since 2006 because of demands for economic growth and job-creation needs through information society-based economic development initiatives. As a consequence, online-only media outlets and online versions of broadcast channels and print newspapers have particularly boomed with a wide array of political information and perspectives to be shared, consumed, and discussed by individuals. For citizens whose political discussions were often marginalized to the safety of the private sphere, online discussion spaces allowed for more autonomous and semi-public political discussions and public opinion formation.

## Diasporic News Consumption during the Arab Spring

The international Arabic-speaking diaspora is estimated to be more than 30 million and is located primarily in Europe (France, Germany, and the United Kingdom), with a few noteworthy populations in North and South America (Brazil, Argentina, and the United States). With significant diasporic minorities in Europe and millions in the Americas now consuming a shared diet of international news, Arab citizens are both transnational and transregional. ICTs and digital media offer their cyber activists new opportunities to gather and disseminate political information produced by the new cohort of news workers. Social change in the Arab Spring was in large part due to this important dynamic of growing media access and networked activists sharing this information. Studies exploring large and small national organizations find that web discussion forums made use of news information to discuss political events and to produce action alerts for interested online citizens to engage locally and transnationally (Nagel and Staeheli 2010). Mass emailing lists allow these individuals to organize and to publicize their activities.

Furthermore, the newly privatized pan-Arab media networks discussed earlier do not operate alone. Western media outlets such as CNN International and the BBC World Service are accessed by Western Arab diasporas, as well as transregional Arab activists. BBC World News' Arabic network was the oldest (launched in 1938) (el Issawi and Baumann 2010) and had the largest budget, broadcasting a 24-hour television channel duplicated online with a large quantity of interactive web content (Cheesman, Nohl, and BBC WS US Elections Study Group 2011). In the Arab diaspora located in the European Union, Arab news consumers combine national television consumption with Arabic language television. Al Jazeera is the most watched network for diasporas originating from the Maghreb region (Morocco, Algeria, and Tunisia) located primarily in France, Spain, and the Netherlands, and they have a more distinct news diet (Slade 2010). A more diverse range of Arab transplants located in Sweden, Germany, and the United Kingdom, on the other hand, consume a combination of BBC Arabic, Al Jazeera, CNN, and Al Arabiya; these individuals have particularly high levels of media literacy and critical evaluations of media content (Camauer 2010).

On the other hand, a closer examination of Arab citizens who consume Western international news services is also revealing: they are primarily located in North Africa and the Middle East (61 percent of all non-Western audiences) (Andersson, Gillespie, and Mackay 2010). The top countries consuming BBC Arabic online information are Egypt, the United States, Saudi Arabia, the United Kingdom, the United Arab Emirates, Germany, and Canada. This audience is relatively young and technologically savvy 25- to 44-year-olds with professional backgrounds and high levels of education. Of the frequently consumed international news content, one third of all news tends to be about the Middle East. Because mobile phones have reached relative ubiquity in developing Arab countries, many individuals reach international news content through mobile phones.

## Citizen Journalism and User-Generated Content as Civic Engagement

It is important to reemphasize here that contemporary Arab media systems are both transnational and transregional. They nurture digital diasporas that connect citizens of Arab countries who do not enjoy free and open political systems. The evolution of broadcast channels entering a post-broadcast era has also led to a boom in online journalism. This has introduced new avenues for the creative consumption of international news content with new repertoires for political action. Sometimes these repertoires are strikingly vivid, but often they come in the form of semi-public online spaces for political discussion and learning about shared experiences and grievances. These new developments are in important ways possible only due to the uniqueness of digital information: multimedia content that is interactive, immediate, and transportable.

The nature of digital news information means that dynamic political information can be found immediately through official outlets (CNN, BBC, Al Jazeera online) as well as through online indexing and search services (Google, Yahoo, MSN). It means that this information can be transported and repackaged by online information consumers to suit their needs, such as discussion and mobilization. Important by-products of these possibilities come in the form of thriving news discussion forums and political blogs. Even in countries with strict digital censorship, such as Egypt and Tunisia, activists were able to organize *because* they had been taking part in identifying and discussing shared grievances and nurturing tactics for political action. Free from the institutional constraints of news organizations, digital activists are free to reshape and repackage news information with their personalized interpretations and motivating messages for sympathetic audiences.

Long before the swelling of the Arab Spring, there were many Arab bloggers and digital activists shaping their tactics with the new international news information made available to them on the web. Dashti has documented the role of online journalism in the 2006 Kuwaiti electoral crisis: while the local press was not able to cover the electoral controversy effectively, Kuwaiti citizens looked online (Dashti 2009). Because offline political discussion could not take place publicly, the online public sphere filled with international news information and free discussion spaces served as the forum to find and express citizen views. These political discussions could have taken place without international news information, but with it, Kuwaitis could fact-check and refute the official statements of political elites. In contrast to Kuwait's moment of political crisis, Al-Saggaf (2006), looking at the Saudi-owned Al Arabiya online, found that Arab online citizens also fact-check news organizations' narratives by responding to articles and discussing issues, as well as expressing their opinions and attacking views by challenging them with evidence found in competing news services. Online discussion spaces found in autonomous news forums or in news organizations' interactive spaces, then, became a vital new semi-public sphere in the Arab world. Al Nashmi et al.

(2010), looking at Kuwaiti, Saudi, Egyptian, and Jordanian online forums, found that almost every news event in 2006 was heavily discussed and debated by Arab internet users.

It is accurate to describe contemporary Arab media systems as both transregional and transnational. This mediascape is also composed of regional journalists who see themselves as Al Jazeera-type change agents, as well as non-Arab international news organizations such as CNN International and BBC Arabic. It includes citizen bloggers and online citizens who consume news information in an interactive and creative way. Since the Web2.0 boom beginning in 2006, this hybrid environment has led to a thriving ecology of transregional Arabic speaking and diverse international digital diasporas composing the Arabic blogosphere. The network study of Arabic language blogs conducted by Etling et al. (2010) has identified some significant clusters. Many of the bloggers are located in the Middle East, but there is a significant "bridge" of English-speaking bloggers that are expatriates from North Africa and the Middle East residing in Western countries. They are political and active consumers of online, international news information. In fact, 46 percent engaged with international news as well as other social and political issues. They also share a high level of inter-linking, but not much external-linking; in other words, they are a cohesive and dynamic group of individuals with shared interests. They frequently rely on online news from BBC, the *Guardian*, CNN, Al Jazeera, the *New York Times*, and other Arab and English news organizations. News-aggregating services are also popular, such as Google News. In contrast to previous concerns of an Arab street, Etling et al. concluded that this is ample evidence of a thriving, networked Arab public sphere:

> It is a political discourse space apparently free of government control. It draws as heavily on peer-produced Web 2.0 resources such as YouTube and Wikipedia as on traditional mainstream media; however, it remains deeply enmeshed in the domestic, pan-Arab, and international news media ecologies. . . . Mainstream news is cited alongside cell phone video shot in the street. Sometimes mainstream media events become the basis for "bottom-up" action, as in the case of the Saudi prince whose on-air criticism of sports announcers sparked mass online outrage. It is a space that members of these societies use to communicate about matters they understand to be of public concern and that potentially require collective action or recognition. (2010, pp. 1240)

# Acting Together: Al Jazeera and Citizen Journalists during the Arab Spring

Despite the diverse and active digital mediascape made possible by the proliferation of social media and broadcast media, it is Al Jazeera English (AJE) that played a significant role in amplifying the distributed and diverse voices of the Arab Spring. Over the past several years, Al Jazeera English has grown rapidly in importance for mediating both transregional and international politics. Over the past several political crises, Al Jazeera English has also learned actively from past challenges and beta-tested strategies for covering dangerous areas. Combining both advantages during the Arab Spring, Al Jazeera was well equipped to navigate the region's political and cultural complexities, feeding coverage about the Arab Spring to the rest of the world; it became the default go-to source on Arab Spring updates for many other organizations, including the *New York Times*, the Huffington Post, Reuters, and Wired.

Since 2008, Al Jazeera English has laid the groundwork for a unique style of storytelling that presents compelling narratives, but also a mix of citizens' voices with political elites. For example, during the 2008 Gaza War, Al Jazeera reporters lost contact with the network's Doha headquarters. Instead of stopping coverage, they turned to mobile phones until live feeds were restored, winning prestigious awards in the process, such as "Best 24 Hour News Programme" at the 48th Monte Carlo Television Festival, and AdBuster's "Broadcaster of the Year" in 2010. Their Gaza coverage won them references such as "the BBC of the [global] South." During the Arab Spring, Secretary of State Clinton applauded Al Jazeera English for outcompeting US news media in offering "real news." While prestigious Western news outlets such as CNN and MSNBC turned to American political commentators for updates about the Arab Spring, Al Jazeera English was securing interviews with Egyptian opposition party leaders and covering minute-by-minute updates through live feeds even in the most contentious and dangerous locations. Reaching more than 150 million households in more than 100 countries worldwide through television, Al Jazeera English's footprint also reaches the Arab digital diaspora, which was an essential ingredient for the digital activists both on the ground in places such as Tahrir Square and their counterparts mobilizing solidarity protests in Europe and North America.

These trends were facilitated through AJE's unique approach toward incorporating digital content and reaching online news consumers. Beyond

AJE's existing regional advantage in North Africa and the Middle East, the network had a number of digital tools and digital strategies to deploy that others did not. As soon as the protests began in Tunisia and cascaded to multiple countries, AJE organized rapid updates and a large influx of news in its live blogs. Unlike other services waiting patiently to verify and double-check information, AJE did both: posting information as it came in onto the live blogs, then doing extended articles and in-focus stories on information that was double-checked and verified. With this combination of rapid reporting and in-depth coverage, a diverse set of viewers' needs was addressed. First, online and offline activists were able to coordinate with a quick understanding of successes, failures, and dangers experienced by others like them in neighboring countries. Second, the 150 million households in 100 countries could learn about a rapidly escalating and complex cascade through AJE's deep coverage.

Another important innovation AJE offered its online viewers was its remarkably open and forward-looking approach toward user-generated content. It is true that AJE journalists have risked their lives to cover dangerous locations. But sometimes the dangers are too high for reporters to cover events effectively. As a route-around during the 2009 Gaza War, Al Jazeera Labs began testing an online citizen journalism application based on the award winning Ushahidi platform, giving citizen journalists on the ground in Gaza a way to document casualties. Between late December 2008 and late January 2009 this platform documented daily casualties, which peaked during the war with more than 40 user-submitted and documented reports. The meta-data from these reports were used to generate maps of the conflict and seed real stories then explored and expanded upon by professional journalists.

AJE also accepted contributions through its YourMedia page, where any citizen could submit stories for coverage and attach raw content giving AJE a Creative Commons License use for rebroadcast in their coverage. The Creative Commons Repository was deployed by AJE during the Gaza War and fed mostly through direct submission by citizens and activists working on the ground. With this repository, AJE encouraged its online supporters with the message that their "videos will be downloaded, shared, remixed, subtitled, and eventually rebroadcasted by users and TV stations across the world" (Andrews 2009).

Riyaad Minty, head of Social Media and AJE Labs, cites that much of the Creative Commons and user-submitted content was redeployed at

Wikipedia by film makers, for remixing music videos; by artists; in video games; for teaching; and by activists and indie media. The recently launched television show "The Stream" is also an important innovation—both a social media community and a daily television program; the creators tap into user-generated content to seek out unheard voices, find new perspectives, and amplify less-covered communities' perspectives both online and through its television show. The founder of the Creative Commons license, Lawrence Lessig, praised AJE's bold approach toward user-generated content, stating, "Al Jazeera is teaching an important lesson about how free speech gets built and supported. By providing a free resource for the world, the network is encouraging wider debate and a richer understanding" (Al Jazeera English 2009).

Al Jazeera English reaches its largest numbers of followers through its satellite shows and television viewership. But in important ways, most viewers find its content online. In countries where AJE was not available on television (such as the United States and parts of Europe), AJE effectively bypassed the telecommunications ban by streaming live content online. In February 2011, Al Jazeera live streamed 24-hour coverage of the Egypt protests through Google TV and its YouTube channel, driving a 2,500 percent increase in traffic to its home website (Lee 2011). The majority of the traffic came from the US viewers, whose opinions have a weight in foreign policy toward the Middle East. Another steady, live source of AJE coverage was through its main Twitter channel and as well as Al Jazeera journalists' individual Twitter channels. For example, during the riots leading up to the Tunisian revolution, journalist Yasmine Ryan's Twitter page became a critical source for organizing and sharing rapid updates about the protests.

Al Jazeera English and other news organizations established since the inception of digital media are more limber in their newswork and more successful in adapting to digital environments saturated with user-generated content than other, traditional media organizations. Al Jazeera English was open to incorporating inspiring examples of citizen journalism, innovative in promoting the use of Creative Commons Licensing, and successful in extracting critical updates from within dangerous regions such as Gaza with creative digital tools. Both new media journalism and young citizen journalists did a lot of work to bring youth activists together, resulting in the unification of these kinds of movements while older, traditional political parties were fragmenting and older news organizations were struggling to adapt to a new political information environment.

# Conclusion: Digitizing the News about the Arab Spring

As an event, the Arab Spring had two primary consequences for the political economy of journalism in the Arab world. First, citizens demonstrated, using social media, that they could make news in creative ways using digital tools and their social networks. Second, Al Jazeera's position in the region as a credible, responsible, and responsive news organization was solidified. News about the Arab Spring came from social media and cell-phone videos uploaded on Facebook, Twitter, Flickr, YouTube, and other sites, but they were effective because pan-Arab satellite networks such as AJE rebroadcast them with amplifying effects that mobilized and enraged regional and international publics.

Indeed, studies of Arab journalists find them favoring regional coverage and explicitly pushing for social change (Pintak and Ginges 2008). In a 2008 survey of Arab journalists, 75 percent identified "encouraging political reform" as the most significant job of a journalist, followed by human rights, with 32 percent believing that a lack of political change was the greatest threat facing the Arab world, not foreign threats, such as US policies. It is telling, then, that Al Jazeera's vision includes a mission "to support the right of the individual to acquire information and strengthen the values of tolerance, democracy and the respect of liberties and human rights." Perhaps more significantly, the growing cohort of Arab journalists also self-identify more with the Muslim world (35 percent) than the Arab region (25 percent) and least with their home country (15 percent) (Pintak 2009), and they "represent a fusing of Muslim and Arab worldviews that is leading the body politic in directions that reinforce a sense of shared consciousness."

One important consequence of this new socialization of journalists is their significant role as cultural intermediaries (Mellor 2008) for Arab publics: from messengers of the state to rebels guiding social change. Indeed, the growth of pan-Arab television has also been credited with the growth of transnational political identification (Nisbet and Myers 2010). But beyond satellite television, social media had a role in supporting a particular kind of identity formation among the young men and women who eventually led the uprisings. Even in countries with relatively few social media users, such as Libya, analysis of Facebook content noted significant identity markers of collectivism, pan-Arab and national pride, but fairly few markers of Islamic affirmation in the cause (Carr et al. 2011).

# Conclusion: Digital Media and the Rhythms of Social Change

By 2012, Egypt and Tunisia had run elections and were drafting fresh constitutions, there were new Parliaments and Cabinets in Morocco and Jordan, with significant commitments to extend franchise. Traditional political actors had been drawn into the movement for popular democracy. Even in constitutional monarchies where ruling families remained in control, a greatly expanded welfare state was the cost of the stability. Several countries are now governed by transitional governments with imperfect constitutions and predatory militaries. It will be years before we can judge the democratic practices of the new governments. But even in countries where Islamism is on the rise, the most viable Islamist leaders are competing in elections and advocating different brands of Islamic constitutionalism.

In this chapter, we build on the multi-stage framework for political change observed during the early aftermath of the Arab Spring (Howard and Hussain 2011) to understand the contextual variables that were in play before it occurred. The most successful cases of sustained and peaceful protest, followed by institutional regime change, were Tunisia and Egypt. Both cases exemplified certain phases: a preparation phase, involving activists' use of digital media across time to build solidarity networks and identify collective identities and goals; an ignition phase involving symbolically powerful moments that ruling elites and regimes intentionally or lazily ignored but that served to galvanize the public; a protest phase, where, by employing offline networks and digital technologies, small groups strategically organized in large numbers; an international buy-in phase, where digital media networks extended the range of local coverage to international broadcast networks; a climax phase where the regime maneuvered strategically or carelessly to appease public dis-content through welfare packages or harsh repressive actions; and finally, a follow-on information warfare phase where various actors, state based and from international civic advocacy networks, compete to shape the future of civil society and information infrastructure that made it possible. But this nar-rative of political change, though generalizable to many Arab Spring cases, does not account for some important variables that were in play or for cases where regimes benefited or did not experience any noticeable liberalization. Weighing multiple political, economic, and cultural conditions, we argue that information infrastructure—especially mobile phone use—consistently ap-pears as one of the key ingredients in parsimonious models behind regime fragility and social movement success. Internet use is relevant in some solu-tion sets, but by causal logic it is actually the absence of internet use that explains low levels of success.

Looking at these important steps toward the first successful large-scale movements for political and economic reform in the Arab world, it is clear that the battle over the use and applicability of information infrastructure became a repeated tool and location for political contention. Though it is tempting to follow this chronology of phases and begin anticipating what is next to come, it is important to recognize that successful uses of digital media across many cases of the Arab world were potentially counterbalanced by important in-stances where digital media, even when available, may not have been very useful. For example, the United Arab Emirates and Qatar boast some of the highest levels of connectivity and e-government development in the Arab world, but these countries experienced hardly any successful offline mobiliza-tion. Additionally, as in Saudi Arabia (and Iran), some regimes were very mas-terful in designing information censorship and management protocols nearing the sophistication shown by China.

In prior observations during the lead up to the Arab Spring movements, we have also observed four key criteria that were being supported by the diffusion of mobile phones and digital media (Hussain and Howard 2012): an increase in the production and consumption of international news (Chapter 1); wide-spread diffusion and use of social networking tools (Chapter 2); the entrench-ment of online civil society; and growing access to include a greater number of political publics, including women and minority ethnic communities (Chapter 3). As evidenced during the Arab Spring, Al Jazeera English, the BBC, and related international news organizations have paved inroads across Arab countries and delivered political information and news countering the state-managed broadcast networks (Chapter 5). Authoritarian regimes that were used to playing closed internal games related to the narratives of corrupt election practices and inability to provide necessary welfare to their citizens are no longer able to do so (Chapter 4).

Furthermore, when periods of political upheaval present themselves, these international news organizations play an important function in spreading the news to sympathetic political diasporas abroad and sometimes encouraging foreign governments to intervene, as in the case of Libya and, less successfully, Syria. This international networking of citizens is amplified by broadcast networks and the successful connectivity made possible by the diffusion of social media tools, like Facebook, YouTube, and Twitter, and it includes average citizens in the shaping and flow of political information. Indeed, citizen journalism videos and blogs were important vehicles for spreading news about self-immolations in Tunisia, Egypt, Saudi Arabia, and Algeria. More formally organized networks of citizens and civic organizations have also led to the entrenchment of civil society, albeit in some cases, mostly online. These civil society groups, like the April 6 Youth Movement in Egypt, and banned but preeminent political parties, like the Muslim Brotherhood, have all successfully used information infrastructure to do political organizing and capacity building *over time*, not simply during the phase of street protests. The April 6 Youth Movement has been active since at least 2008, and the Muslim Brotherhood has built a massive online blogging and news production ecology outweighing any other Egyptian party or movement. Last, and especially in the case of women in the Middle East, many, including but not limited to, feminist movements, have expanded the range of political inclusion from suffrage rights to driving, particularly in Saudi Arabia—and they have done so through online advocacy movements and awareness campaigns. Media have been particularly important to "pink hijabis," who integrate their faith with the pursuit of women's rights by circulating films about female genital mutilation to friends and family, organizing workshops about technology strategies, and learning about successful digital strategies from like-minded groups in other countries (Wright 2011). This short list of key changes in the social makeup of societies in closed authoritarian regimes is evidence of locations where state and society relations have been forever altered (Migdal, Kohli, and Shue 1994). One of the key ingredients facilitating them has been the *long-term* diffusion and use of digital media (Howard 2010).

## Fuzzy Logic

In the analytical discourse so far, there are two ways of describing the causes and consequences of the Arab Spring. The first analytical frame is to identify the things that make a country susceptible to protests, or fragile when faced with a popular uprising. The second is to identify the things that might explain a successful uprising. Rather than looking for simple or singular causal explanations for what made a country susceptible to popular uprisings or what allowed a popular uprising to achieve its goals, we should observe that there are complex causal patterns, or even several "causal recipes" that would provide analytical purchase over several sets of cases. Moreover, knowing what we now know about social movements and regime change, it makes most sense to look for "conjoined causal conditions," the set of multiple indicators that together provide a fulfilling narrative for understanding political outcomes.

There have been numerous single-country case studies in which ICTs have been part of the contemporary narrative of both democratic entrenchment and persistent authoritarianism. The comparative perspective taken in our investigation is not limited to the standard cases or even to situations that stand out as incidents of technology-driven, enhanced, or enabled regime change. Instead our comparative perspective embraces situations in which information technologies had little to no role in democratic promotion, those in which information technologies were carefully used by authoritarian elites to become better bullies, and situations in which information technologies played a critical role in sudden democratic transitions. Thus, the comparative approach is anathema to those who would generalize from singular studies in which information technologies had a central role in a grand democratization project and those who would generalize by only relying on statistical models of international data on government effectiveness in terms of internet penetration.

Methodologically, the comparative approach is powerful and productive in that it confronts theory with data. Sometimes this approach is called "set-theoretic" in that attention is given to consistent similarities or differences across a set of cases, especially the causally relevant commonalities uniformly present in a given set of cases (Byrne and Ragin 2009). The set of cases at hand is the population of Arab countries with large Muslim communities, and there are at least 22 of these. The argument of our investigation is that in recent years, information technologies have opened up new paths to democratization and the entrenchment of civil society in many Arab countries.

Large-N quantitative researchers often turn "democratization" into an indicator for which the Western democracies are the standard. In our set-theoretic approach, we assume that democratization among these 22 countries is best calibrated according to more grounded standards, set by countries such as Lebanon at the high end, and Saudi Arabia at the low end. This calibration does not preclude the theoretical possibility of an Islamic democratic ideal type. So a grounded approach does assume that healthy, functional Muslim democracies may not look like Western democracies. Set-theoretic reasoning allows for fine gradations in the degree of membership in the set of successful democratic outcomes, and it requires evidence about each country's degree of membership in the set of countries that have experienced democratic transition or entrenchment during or since the Arab Spring.

Moreover, a set-theoretic explanation of the role of ICTs in contemporary democratization requires that we identify a consistent set of causal relations between technology diffusion and political liberalization outcomes. To construct this explanation requires fuzzy set logic, which does not explain variation in a sample through reductive correlational statistics. Instead, fuzzy set logic produces general knowledge about the role of information technology in contemporary democratic transitions through the accumulated experience of particular countries where rapid technology diffusion among political actors such as the state, parties, journalists, and civic groups has an observed impact on the domestic balance of power, the opportunity structure for social mobilization, or the "cognitive liberation" of citizenry.

Fuzzy set logic offers general knowledge through the strategy of looking for shared causal conditions across multiple instances of the same outcome—sometimes called "selecting on the dependent variable." For large-N, quantitative, and variable oriented researchers, this strategy is unacceptable because neither the outcome nor the shared causal conditions vary across the cases (King, Keohane, and Verba 1994). However, the strategy of selecting on the dependent variable is useful if researchers are interested in studying necessary conditions (Ragin 1987). Perhaps most important, this strategy is most useful when developing theory grounded in the observed, real-world experience of democratization in the Arab-Muslim communities of the developing world rather than deploying theory privileging null, hypothetical, and unobserved cases.

The qualitative and quantitative empirical evidence reviewed thus far lends itself to a set-theoretic argument, because the evidence reveals that many of the countries experiencing protests have high levels of ICT diffusion, and almost all experienced significant changes in their political systems and/or economic welfare policies. Our claim is based on the parsimoniously summarized relations between properties and cases rather than modest correlations between technology diffusion and democratization. Examining cases with the same causal conditions to see if they also share the democratization outcome is appropriate for identifying sufficient conditions, and sufficient conditions often appear as combinations of conditions. Identifying the causal conditions shared by cases that have democratized is appropriate for identifying the necessary conditions of democratization. In other words, if information technologies and infrastructure are a sufficient cause of democratization, then the presence of information technologies implies the presence of democratization (though democratization does not imply the presence of information technologies).

On the other hand, if a sophisticated information management and censorship infrastructure is a necessary cause of no political change, then the presence of no democratic outcome implies the presence of a strong censorship regime. It is possible that there are several recipes for contemporary democratization, and many possible ingredients and combinations of ingredients. One way to assemble the accumulated country experience is by comparing the recent histories of countries that share the common outcome of a significant period of democratic transition or entrenchment, such as in the Arab Spring. Analyzing the relationships in this set-theoretic manner exposes the key ingredients for democratization. Moreover, treating the institutional outcomes as fuzzy-sets avoids selecting cases based on the outcome because countries will actually vary in their degree of membership in the set displaying democratic transition or entrenchment. Set theory allows us to examine cases with the same causal conditions to see if they also share the same outcome. More important, if we assume that there is not just one recipe for contemporary democratization, but several, we can use fuzzy set analysis to identify combinations of causal conditions that share the same outcome.

## Fuzzy Variables

Several contextual factors may have exacerbated or mitigated the causal role of particular aspects of technology diffusion, and reducing the set of causal attributes to a few important ones must also respect the significant diversity among these countries. The cases involved in the Arab Spring differ in important ways, yet there may still be causal patterns and shared attributes that explain membership in the set of countries that have or have not democratized. Along with the impact of technology diffusion on the system of political communication involving states, journalists, political parties, civil society groups, and cultural elites, additional contextual conditions should also be evaluated on a case-by-case basis, and they vary widely across the region.

Average incomes vary among countries and are measured as GDP per capita (adjusted for purchasing power parity), a measure that accounts for the large diversity in the access to wealth by citizens. Among other things, this indicator is useful for contextualizing the relative cost of living and inflation rates in countries rather than distorting the real differences in income by countries. The high end of this scale includes rich countries like Qatar, the UAE, Kuwait, and Bahrain (average range of $20,000–$70,000); the low end includes countries like Djibouti, Mauritania, Iraq, and Somalia (average range of $200–$1,000). Equitable distribution of wealth is also a key indicator often measured as Gini coefficients for income distribution. This measure accounts for the wide range of access to wealth by differing members of Arab societies. The distribution of wealth in many Arab countries is relatively unequal—the upper half of more equally distributed wealth in societies includes cases like Lebanon and Qatar, and the lower half of *un*equally distributed wealth includes extreme cases like the UAE and Egypt. Many commentators have noted that access to jobs may have been a primary source of existing discontent in many countries, particularly Tunisia (14 percent) and Yemen (15 percent), but cases on the lower end, including Saudi Arabia (5 percent) and Kuwait (1 percent) also experienced political discontent and protests. Levels of unemployment are useful to include because whether levels of unemployment were a central factor in nurturing support for political and economic change must be examined comparatively in the recipes for democratic political change.

Beyond economic inequality, general population measures are important for understanding the macro social contexts of Arab societies undergoing profound political and social change: the total population, the proportion of urban population of societies (where most digital connectivity is located), and the proportion of those societies that is under the age of 25 (a demographic often cited as most politically disenfranchised and enraged). Qatar and Kuwait are the most urbanized (96–98 percent) and are counterbalanced by Yemen and Somalia (32–38 percent). Yemen and Somalia also have the largest proportion of young citizens (45 percent), while Qatar and Kuwait have the smallest (16–23 percent). When considering the total mass of citizenry, Qatar and Kuwait are well below 10 million, and both Yemen and Somalia are well over. Understanding the dynamic relationships between the total population and critical proportions of young disenfranchised citizens residing in connected urban hubs will provide important context for unpacking the recipes for political change.

Additionally, one of the most consistent variables predicting a regime's capacity to hold out from making a meaningful political transition has been the amount of natural resources it can utilize to buffer its security apparatuses or quell discontent over distributions of wealth. In the Arab Middle East, many countries, particularly those in the Gulf Cooperation Council, export vast volumes of crude oil and enjoy a significant backing from the international system whose foreign policy interests prioritize regional stability over the unpredictable democratic transition of ailing authoritarians. To account for this significant variable, we included countries' levels of oil production and shares in the global oil resources available. Saudi Arabia, the UAE, and Kuwait ranked highest.

Digital connectivity and access to information infrastructure are the central variables being investigated in relation to other variables. Here, we observe digital connectivity through the diffusion of mobile and internet telephony. Interestingly, more than half of Arab countries have mobile penetration well over 100 percent. These countries include Tunisia (106 percent), Bahrain (124 percent), and Saudi Arabia (188 percent). The other half are below 100 percent and include Egypt (87 percent), Syria (68 percent), and Yemen (46 percent). Patterns of internet diffusion share similar properties, but are somewhat lower than mobile penetration. Countries with 25 percent or more internet access include Saudi Arabia (27 percent), Tunisia (34 percent), and Bahrain (54 percent). Countries with 25 percent or less internet access include Libya (5 percent), Yemen (10 percent), and Egypt (15 percent). To counterbalance digital access and shared connectivity, many regimes in the Arab world have instituted censorship mechanisms that range widely in levels of sophistication. As noted earlier, a few countries have very sophisticated monitoring and management systems, including Saudi Arabia, Bahrain, and the UAE. On the other hand, some regimes, including Algeria, Egypt, and Libya, were either sloppy or unable to monitor activity. To examine these cases comparatively we created an index combining the OpenNet Initiative's monitoring of countries that had instituted *no filtering*, or a range of *selective*, *substantial*, and *pervasive* filtering on content for *political*, *social*, *security* reasons or used *automated tools* to do so. Our index combines these multiple dimensions of censorship and sophistication in filtering to assess the overall censorship regime's capacity for managing new information infrastructure.

Last, because our key research questions deal with the contextual factors and variables at play during the Arab Spring, many of our predictive variables listed above come from the latest data points available at or just before the protest periods. However, our overall objective in this investigation was to identify causal recipes that best predict the widest range of democracy promoting outcomes from the Arab Spring. Therefore, our outcome variable measures countries on a scale from ideal cases of peaceful democratic regime change (Egypt and Tunisia), followed by major political and economic concessions (Oman and Saudi Arabia), followed by major political concessions only (Kuwait and Jordan), followed by economic concessions only (Lebanon and Bahrain), and last, countries that reached bloody civil wars and/or violent stalemates with ruling elites (Libya and Syria). The fuzzy ranks for this variable took into account the detailed qualitative information for each case, including the longevity of protest, numbers of killed and injured citizens, types of meaningful political concessions, and levels of economic redistributions of wealth. The outcome variables were created from the data presented in Tables I.1 and I.2.

In each case and variable, the data used came from 2011 or the best available year (2005 to 2010). When the data taken from large datasets were incomplete, supplementary data from secondary sources were sought and double checked with cooperating sources. Patching these gaps by hand significantly reduced the number of missing cases and provided for a more robust and meaningful fuzzy ranking system. Preparing data for treatment as a fuzzy set required several steps. First, we computed indices for causal attributes analyzed in each chapter and then we computed the indices for additional context variables often recommended by the literature on democratization in the developing world and the latest scholarly and policy reports since the Arab Spring. Then we calibrated the indices, a process that evens out the distribution of cases between the thresholds for full inclusion in each set, full exclusion from the set, and the crossover point at which cases go from being partially in the set to being partially out of the set.

For example, among the 22 countries there are a few very populated countries and many countries with a small population. Egypt and Saudi Arabia are at the top of this set, and obviously help define the category of "populated country." In fact, Egypt has such a large population that if the set were left uncalibrated, Tunisia and Syria would be barely in the set, and most of the countries would be fully out of the set. Yet the important attribute is that some countries are comparatively more populated than others, so calibration makes the differences between the populous countries more comparable to those between smaller countries. The very populated countries still define the set by being almost full members, while the rest of the cases get indexed by their degrees of membership in the set. In this case, the threshold value for full membership in the set of populated countries is established just below the actual population of Iraq. At the lowest points in the curve are countries such as Bahrain, Qatar, and Oman, and these are definitely not very populated countries. So the threshold for full exclusion is set at 3 million people because these countries have even smaller populations than that. The crossover threshold has been set at 10 million people, which roughly splits countries into two groups. Since Somalia and Tunisia have barely 10 million citizens, these two countries are just barely in the category of "populated country."

The recalibration around these thresholds allows for fuzzy set values that more meaningfully reveal the degree to which each country can be included in the theoretical set of populated countries. As another example, for membership in the category of countries with a strong censorship regime, the threshold for full membership is defined as regimes that pervasively or substantially filter at least two categories measured by the Open Net Initiative (political, social, security, or tools). Saudi Arabia, Bahrain, and the UAE all fall comfortably into full inclusion into this category. Countries that had a very unsophisticated political information management regime had no functional ability to monitor and filter online content. Algeria, Egypt, and Lebanon all fall comfortably into the fully excluded category. Syria, Kuwait, and Oman are barely included because they do all, some, or no filtering, and none was robust enough to "pervasively" or "substantially" filter on two or more of the four filtering categories.

In addition, fuzzy calibrations allow researchers to put comparative knowledge to work to complete incomplete datasets. In this study, there were four hand calibrations. There were no censorship scores for Djibouti, Mauritania, and Somalia, but secondary sources suggest that the level of censorship in Djibouti was much like that of Kuwait, that the level of censorship in Mauritania was higher than Lebanon's but not as a high as Jordan's, and that the level of censorship in Somalia was almost as high as that in Saudi Arabia. The final hand calibration involved designating a Polity score for Somalia. Polity IV identifies Somalia as a failed state in 2010. This case is not likely to teach us much about a theoretical relationship between political institutions, technology diffusion, and popular movements for democracy, so it was given a fuzzy score of 0.50. This is a special score designating a case that is neither in nor out of the theoretical set of democracies. A score of 0.51 would mean that a country is very slightly in the theoretical set of democracies, and a score of 0.49 would mean that a country is just out of such a set. But the transition score signals that if this variable is important, Somalia is not a good instance.[1]

## Fuzzy Recipes for Fragility and Success

Table C.1 presents two of the parsimonious models with the best balance of case coverage and solution consistency. Certainly, there are more complex formulations of conditions that would also explain the susceptibility of a regime to a popular uprising, or the chances such an uprising would be successful. Moreover, each case could be described with a unique combination of causal factors. The combinations reported here are not the only plausible ones, but they do cover the widest spectrum of Arab experience around the developing world, and the cases are largely consistent with causal conditions for democratic outcomes. Coverage refers to the percentage of cases explained by that recipe.

Consistency refers to the degree to which cases adhere to a particular causal recipe. As in many statistical procedures, the research proceeds by examining a variety of models. In testing out all of the plausible causal variables, urbanization and youth unemployment rarely appeared in parsimonious explanations. These variables were dropped in the analysis of regime fragility. Having high levels of income but poor internet diffusion and low Gini scores made regimes vulnerable to public demonstrations, and Libya, Algeria, and Saudi Arabia are the best examples of how this causal combination resulted in regime sensitivity. A second parsimonious explanation is that regimes with high levels of unemployment, significant mobile phone use, and low levels of internet censorship also made regimes sensitive—Libya and Oman are the best instances of this causal relationship.

Whereas there were multiple conjoined causal recipes for regime fragility, and the two with highest levels of consistency were presented in Table C.2, there was a relatively short and complete parsimonious solution for the analysis of social movement success. This analysis, presented in Table C.2, yielded three causal recipes, which altogether covered two thirds of the cases with four fifths consistency. Here mobile phones, not internet use, appeared

*Table C.1*   **Two Parsimonious Models Explaining Regime Fragility**

| Variables Included | Causal Recipe | Raw Coverage | Unique Coverage | Consistency | Best Instances |
|---|---|---|---|---|---|
| Average income, unemployment rate, internet and mobile phone penetration rates, levels of censorship, size of the youth bulge, wealth distribution, economic dependence on fuel exports, regime type in 2010 | Relatively high average levels of income, where the wealth is evenly distributed, and internet use is very low | 0.44 | 0.00 | 0.97 | Libya (0.58,0.95), Algeria (0.58,0.53), Saudi (0.53,0.63) |
| | Relatively high levels of unemployment, with many mobile phone users and not much regime censorship | 0.50 | 0.00 | 0.98 | Libya (0.81,0.95), Oman (0.58,0.74) |

Note: The consistency cutoff for the first causal recipe was set at 1.00, and the cutoff for the second recipe was set at 0.96.

in several solution sets, and Jordan, Tunisia, and Morocco were the best instances of the conjoined causal relationships. Altogether, these three parsimonious recipes form a solution set with good coverage (0.64) and good consistency (0.79).

# The Causes of Democracy's Fourth Wave

What has happened online over the past several months, and what tools and technological structures facilitated the initial ignition of mass protest? What long-term preludes in information society development were necessary for this to happen? Are digital media simply a new "tool" for social protest, or does more need to be said about the modern character of social protest, the contemporary organizational form of civic unrest, or the changing opportunity

*Table C.2*   **Parsimonious Causal Solution Explaining Social Movement Success**

| Variables Included | Causal Recipe | Raw Coverage | Unique Coverage | Consistency | Best Instances |
|---|---|---|---|---|---|
| Average income, general and youth unemployment rate, internet and mobile phone penetration rates, levels of censorship, urbanization, size of the youth bulge, wealth distribution, economic dependence on fuel exports, regime type in 2010 | Relatively high rates of mobile phone use in countries not dependent on fuel exports | 0.53 | 0.08 | 0.83 | Jordan (0.63,0.58), Tunisia (0.58,0.95), Morocco (0.53,0.58) |
| | Relatively high rates of mobile phone use in countries with lower urbanization rates | 0.52 | 0.02 | 0.88 | Jordan (0.63,0.58), Morocco (0.53,0.58) |
| | Relatively low rates of unemployment, in countries with lower urbanization rates and wealth is more concentrated | 0.44 | 0.03 | 0.86 | Morocco (0.63,0.58), Jordan (0.53,0.58) |

*Note*: The consistency cutoff for the solution set was 1.00.

structure for public dissent? How or to what extent were regimes ready or not ready to deal with unexpected periods of galvanized discontent? Did regime sophistication in managing information infrastructure translate meaningfully to limiting the capacity of civil society to operate and organize?

To answer these questions, we have examined the narrative arc of how digital media changed the tactics for democratization movements *during* the Arab Spring, and how new information and communication technologies played a major role in the organization of street protests. First, many of the countries that experienced long and sustained movements of protest had preexisting political publics that had long been wired and developed tech-savvy civil society groups based both within the region and across borders. In these moments of political crisis, multinational technology firms also played a critical role, where some were constructive in providing activists the tools to create action opportunities. Others, when pressured by dictators and authoritarian regimes, sometimes played into the hands of political suppression. It is difficult to say whether the revolutions would or would not have happened without digital media. Indeed, other sociological factors, such as widespread poverty and governmental ineptitude, had created the conditions for extensive public anger. However, the networks of people who did mobilize did so with the direct application, initiation, and coordination of digital media tools. Counterfactual scenarios are important, but the overwhelming evidence of what did happen concretely illustrates that the patterns of political change in these protests were digitally enabled, both in the short term, but also over time since the early 2000s.

For scholars of social movements and collective action, there are several things in these examples that should be considered more centrally: the distributed leadership of protest organizers, the core groups of elite publics (literate, middle-class, youth, women, and technocrats) that were relatively quick in joining them, and the important role that international news organizations played in giving them the critical voice and global exposure that helped stave off overtly violent reactions from their repressive regimes. We can say more than that the internet changed the way political actors communicated—social movements and collective action networks shared strategies for direct political action, created regional and international news events that drew attention and sympathy from neighboring countries, and inspired others to join and celebrate their causes. One of the key reasons we must turn our attention to the role of information technology is that citizens themselves have expressed and celebrated its role and now consider access to digital media a core nation-building resource.

Subsequently, we must also consider the years leading up to the Arab Spring and the diffusion of digital media, in the form of mobile phones, personal computers, and software applications over time. These technologies and their applications have significantly impacted the political communication systems and their relationships to civil society organizations. First, mobile telephony, in the form of small and affordable consumer-based communication devices, have allowed regular citizens to bear witness, record, and disseminate acts of injustice and repression by their ruling elites and their security agencies.

In important ways, authoritarian regimes holding phony elections also gained widespread infamy, particularly in the Egyptian elections of 2005, when Mubarak's party won 89 percent of the vote. Mobile videos uploaded to

YouTube and other video sharing cites disseminated actual footage of vote counting and rigging. Second, over the last five years, Al Jazeera became a functionally independent *regional* news organization, and with the addition of the English-language network in 2006, an international powerhouse that illuminated the accusations, criticisms, and failures of autocrats. Third, widespread internet access, though limited to middle-class urban-dwellers, offered everyday citizens the opportunity to synthesize social networks with broadcast networks to communicate and engage with political issues. Together, these long-term trends mean that information infrastructure helped decentralize state power, especially regimes that were not quick enough to adapt their management strategies to regulate these new political information spaces.

We have also argued that digital media were very important during the short-term cascade of street protests across the region. For example, we know that online conversations spiked *before* major events on the ground in both cases, as well as many others, across many of the Arab Spring cases. This was possible because social media provided the structural antecedents for democratic ideas to spread across borders, through informal networks of families, friends, and interested onlookers. The intensity of political conversations that took place preceding major street protests supports the idea that virtual networks materialized before street protest networks. For example, detailed maps and guides were widely available before protests began and provided would-be participants with strategies and nonviolent goals to sustain periods of dissent that disabled authoritarian regimes' past coercion and suppression techniques. Indeed, Facebook pages and Twitter conversations were essential for designing and trying out new strategies as events took place on the ground. Political blogospheres, many based nationally but others also based more regionally, brought together political diaspora communities from France, the United Kingdom, and other Western democratic countries (Etling et al. 2010). The ability to produce and consume political content was important because it created a sense of shared grievances and strong political efficacy that had not led to such sizable, diverse, and quick mobilization before the Arab Spring.

Despite the ample evidence illustrating the role of digital media in the Arab Spring, it would be a mistake to suggest the democratic potential of information technologies without considering the important roles that regimes play in managing or limiting their applications. Indeed, there are several regimes that have very sophisticated strategies to effectively co-opt or coerce technology providers. One of the key threats to authoritarian regimes is elite defection. Therefore, some regimes, like Saudi Arabia and the UAE, followed a closely guarded and systematic strategy to monitor and punish a variety of autonomous attempts at online political engagement. Others, like Egypt and Jordan, tolerated such incidents by assuming that some political dissatisfaction could be ventilated online and therefore not materialize substantively offline. When this dissatisfaction did eventually spill over, unfriendly regimes took a range of measures to suppress the political application of digital media. During extreme circumstances, entire global information networks were taken offline. This strategy caused street protests to increase in numbers, especially in Egypt, where individuals turned to traditional institutions to find each other, such as after Friday prayer congregations in Cairo. Disconnecting large information networks also caused regimes to lose millions of dollars on global financial transactions taking place in the world economy. This was the case in Egypt, which lost $18 million USD per day (nearly $90 million USD in total) after turning off mobile and digital networks.

Digital media had a causal role in the Arab Spring in that they provided the fundamental infrastructure for social movements and collective action, a process Bennett and Segerberg (2012) call "connective action." In the first few weeks of protest in each country, the generation of people in the streets—and its leadership—was clearly not interested in the three major models of political Islam. These social movements were not seeking to replace secular dictatorships with Al Qaeda's Salafi Jihadism, Iran's Shiite theocracy, or Saudi's rigid Wahhabism (Wright 2011). Instead, these mostly cosmopolitan and younger generations of mobilizers felt disenfranchised by their political systems, saw vast losses in the poor management of national economies and development, and, most important, voiced a consistent and widely shared narrative of common grievances—a narrative which they learned about from each other and co-wrote on the digital spaces of political writing and venting on blogs, videos shared on Facebook and Twitter, and comment board discussions on international news sites like Al Jazeera and the BBC.

The causes of revolution are always complex, and the conditions under which revolts succeed rare. As Goldstone (2011) observes, for a revolution to succeed, the government must seem so unjust and inept that it is viewed as a threat to the nation's future. A country's combined social, economic, and military elites must be alienated from the state. This happened in Egypt and Tunisia, was slow to happen in Libya and Syria, and did not happen in Bahrain and Saudi Arabia. A regime's opponents must also build consensus across a broad swath of the population, crossing ethnic, religious, and class groups, which in several Arab Spring countries was made possible by digital networks. Finally international powers must either refuse to step in and defend the government or they must constrain the government from defending itself too ruthlessly—both roles which have been played by Western powers at critical moments, but not in all (Goldstone 2011).

The Arab Spring, then, is historically unique because it is the first set of political upheavals in which all of these things were digitally mediated. Digital media allowed local citizens access to international broadcast networks, networks that were then used by online civil society organizations to lobby advocacy campaigns regionally by Arab and Western support groups like AccessNow and the Electronic Frontier Foundation in securing information infrastructure and combating regimes' attempts at committing overt violence and censoring coverage of human rights atrocities. When the internet went down in Egypt, Mubarak also revoked satellite broadcast licenses. As a response, Google began streaming Al Jazeera English directly to YouTube.

Many of the dictators who have held on to power in the Middle East and North Africa have done so by telling their population, their neighbors, and the international community that they were the guardians against Islamist revolution. And many of these networked individuals showed a lack of interest in the political Islamist frameworks of previous generations (Bayat 2007). Some Islamist parties may have benefited from the Arab Spring, as in the aftermath of Tunisia and Egypt, but they did not inspire the uprisings. In fact, they have categorically hesitated to join them till victory and political change was close to a real possibility. Among the countries in the region, those with high rates of technology diffusion and a significant, tech-savvy, and young civil society were the ones where the Arab Spring was most successful, along with regimes that had not mastered the art of managing information infrastructure. The countries with the lowest rates of technology diffusion, or a fragmented civil society with few technology resources, had less successful uprisings. Some of these later countries, including Libya, Syria, and Yemen, did experience extended civil war, but the inciting incidents of political strife, again, were digitally mediated. On the whole, however, the role of digital media in the political unrest of these countries was not as pronounced as it was in Tunisia, Egypt, and Morocco, all of which experienced major political concessions ranging from democratic regime changes or the lifting of political sanctions and replacement of ruling elites.

The argument devaluing the complex causal role of digital media in the Arab Spring is often made through the simple claim that it is people on the streets and their grievances that constitute political revolution. Pundits have made this claim in different ways. Several, including Gladwell, Rosenberg, and Friedman, argue that while Facebook and Twitter may have their place in social change, real revolutions take place on the ground (Gladwell 2010). Rosenberg wrote that the biggest obstacle in using social media for political change is that "people need those personal connections in order to get them to take action—especially if action is risky and difficult" (Rosenberg 2011). For Friedman, "what brought Hosni Mubarak down was not Facebook and it was not Twitter. It was a million people in the streets, ready to die for what they believed in" (Friedman 2011). It is true that Facebook and Twitter were not singular *causes* of revolutions, but it is also silly to ignore the fact that the careful and strategic uses of digital media to network regional publics, along with international support networks, have empowered activists in new ways. These have led to some of the largest protests this decade in Iran, the temporary lifting of the Egyptian blockade on Gaza, and the popular movements that ended the decades long rule of Mubarak and Ben Ali. Digital media had a causal role in the Arab Spring in the sense that they provided the very infrastructure that created deep communication ties and organizational capacity in groups of activists before the major protests took place and while street protests were being formalized. Indeed, it was because of those well-developed, digital networks that civic leaders so successfully activated such large numbers of people to protest.

Social media are the reason we have such good documentation of events. More important, they are the reason that Egyptians had such excellent live coverage of what was going on in Tunisia, and also the reason that Moroccans, Jordanians, and Yemenis had coverage of what was going on in Egypt, just as Libyans and Syrians had coverage of what was going on in those countries, and so on. In other words, it was social media that brought the narrative of successful social protest across multiple, previously closed, media regimes. When things did not go well, as in the case of Bahrain and Libya, activists in the continuing cascade took note and applied these lessons—just as authoritarian regimes, like Syria and Bahrain, have made interesting moves like opening up previously embargoed digital networks to better monitor the strategies and activities of protestors. The Syrian government also very quickly developed a digital counterinsurgency strategy, effectively intimidating that country's activists (one of the region's largest online civil societies) from using social media in a systematic way for organizing. For the most part, it was physical intimidation that discouraged activists from communicating about their political activity on Facebook. But the authoritarian regime also invested in its social media strategy by actively employing people to create pro-government content to distribute over social media networks.

Perhaps the most compelling reason for not dismissing the important causal role of digital media in the Arab Spring is that the traditional analysis, privileging other factors, yields uncompelling explanations (Gause, 2011). For example, *The Economist* magazine built an index of how press freedom, corruption, democratic institutions, income, the youth bulge, and years of authoritarian rule might predict the vulnerabilities of particular regimes. This index used many of the variables that traditional social media theorists also consider important—suggesting that Yemen, Libya, Syria, and Iraq were the most vulnerable. Yet they are neither the inciting nor defining cases of the Arab Spring. Yemen, Libya, and Syria had a small elite of technology activists who helped spread the word of successful rebellion in other countries, but the tough authoritarian regimes responded quickly and forcefully and with their own digital media strategy. These countries descended into months of civil strife and did not see a rapid regime transition. The countries that experienced rapid regime collapse or where regimes made major concessions did not appear particularly vulnerable—for example, Egypt and Tunisia, and Saudi Arabia and Morocco, respectively.

It is wrong-headed to debate how many bloggers it takes to make a democracy. But there is little doubt that, altogether, social media and information infrastructure make useful contributions toward social movement organizing and the mobilization of popular protest. A peripheral look at counts of media use and digital diffusion reveals that the countries experiencing the most dramatic changes had low overall percentages of social media use (Mourtada and Salem 2011). But limiting the analysis to aggregate indicators precludes the possibility of telling a more complex, causal story. Moreover, if there is anything to the analytical frame of networks, the use of important media by a few important nodes of users could be exceptionally consequential. This is why, to unpack the complexities of the Arab Spring, we must employ analytic approaches that make possible the examination of complex social systems that constitute the overall aggregate of state-based cases. Street protests were the most challenging manifestations of political opposition for each regime's security forces, and they were certainly bolstered by decades-long economic and political disenfranchisement of their citizens. Yet the millions of individuals on the streets of capital cities around the region were not disconnected individuals.

In fact, the opposite is true. These protesters were very connected, in groups and networks. Not every Tunisian and Egyptian had access to a computer. But mobile phones were the key mediating instrument bridging communication gaps: they could be easily carried and concealed, could often be used to record and upload photos and videos, and could be recharged in the street. Given the high rates of mobile phone use, especially in the dense urban centers, it is safe to say that each person at the protests either had a mobile phone or was part of a group in which there were several mobile civic journalists and bloggers (see Figure C.1). Before the Arab Spring, most social movement theorists had landed on a straightforward way of describing the importance of digital media. Digital media affected the costs and benefits of action, the opportunities and constraints on actor commitment, and was one of many resources available to activist leaders (Earl and Kimport 2011). In Bimber's account, "socio-technological devices do not determine political outcomes, but simply alter the matrix of opportunities and costs associated with intermediation, mobilization and the organization of politics" (Bimber 2003, p. 231).

*Figure C.1*  Mobile Charging Station in Tahrir Square. (© Alisdare Hickson)

# The Digital Scaffolding for Building a Modern Civil Society

What might have made some regimes more susceptible than others to popular uprisings, and what might explain the relative successes of some movements more than others? What role does information technology have in the modern recipe for democratization? Weighing multiple political, economic, and cultural conditions, we find that information infrastructure—especially mobile phone use—consistently appears as one of the key ingredients in parsimonious models for the conjoined combinations of causes behind regime fragility and social movement success. Internet use is relevant in some solution sets, but by causal logic it is actually the absence of internet use that explains low levels of success.

In every single case, the inciting incidents of the Arab Spring were digitally mediated in some way. Information infrastructure, in the form of mobile phones, personal computers, and social media, were part of the causal story we must tell about the Arab Spring. People were inspired to protest for many different and always personal reasons. Information technologies mediated that inspiration, such that the revolutions followed each other by a few weeks and had notably similar patterns. Certainly there were different political outcomes, but that does not diminish the important role of digital media in the Arab Spring. But even more important, this investigation has illustrated that countries that do not have a civil society equipped with digital scaffolding are much less likely to experience popular movements for democracy than are countries with such an infrastructure—an observation we are able to make only by accounting for the constellation of causal variables that existed *before* the street protests began, not simply the short-term uses of digital technologies during the brief period of political upheaval.

Perhaps some of the best evidence that digital media altered the system of political communication in several countries is in the way political candidates have recently campaigned for office, emboldened by successful digital tactics, and have continued to use information technologies in running for office. In both Egypt and Tunisia, the initial rounds of elections were notable for the way candidates wooed voters with social media strategies. Interacting with voters face to face was most important for reaching the many new voters who were not online and had little experience with campaign politics (Saleh 2011). But competitive candidates also took to the internet, and independent candidates not allied with Islamist parties, such as Mohammed El Baradei in Egypt, also relied heavily on Facebook to activate networks of supporters. Digital media have had a crucial causal role in the formation, enunciation, and activation of coordinated opposition in several countries in North Arica and the Middle East. Now there is more evidence to suggest that this information infrastructure continues to be important after the dictators have fallen—further supporting the need to develop our theories to go beyond seeking linear relationships and to look for parsimonious recipes grounded in limited but real case contexts.

This chapter offers a transportable framework that may describe the staging of contemporary, digitally mediated social change. Digital media ignited popular uprising for democracy across the region, but digital media had for several years served as the scaffolding over which civil society had grown. These media were tools for social protest, but tools that shaped the character of social protest, the contemporary organizational form of civic unrest, and the changing opportunity structure for public dissent. Digital and social media allowed more people in the region to be involved in the production and consumption of international news, to solidify their own social networks using digital applications, to entrench online civil society groups that nurtured new political publics and involved women and minority ethnic communities in new forms of political communication. Several international news agencies delivered political news and information that authoritarian regimes could only clumsily block.

We also offered a six-stage model of protest mobilization: a capacity-building phase that involves the diffusion and entrenchment of digital media over many years in local and diasporic communities; a preparation phase that involves activists learning to use digital media in creative ways to find each other, build solidarity around shared grievances, and identify collective political goals; an ignition phase that involves some inciting incident, usually ignored by mainstream, state-controlled media, that enrages the public and is leveraged by civil society groups; a phase of street protests that are coordinated digitally; a phase of international buy-in, during which digital media are used to draw in international governments, global diasporas, and overseas news agencies; a climax phase in which the state either cracks down, protesters and elites reach a stalemate, or public demands are met; and then a final denouement of a post-protest information war between winners and losers in social change. The countries with the lowest rates of technology diffusion, or a fragmented civil society with few technology resources, had less successful uprisings. But in every single case, the inciting incidents of the Arab Spring were digitally mediated. In this way, mobile phones, personal computers, and social media are part of the causal story we must tell about this period. Certainly there were different political outcomes, but that does not diminish the important role of digital media in the Arab Spring.

# Notes

## Acknowledgments

1. Copyright © 2011 National Endowment for Democracy and The Johns Hopkins University Press. This article first appeared in *Journal of Democracy* 22.3 (2011): 35–48. Reprinted with permission by The Johns Hopkins University Press.

## Chapter 3

1. Demographic data from the CIA World Factbook and World Bank's World Development Indicators database. Technology use data from the International Telecommunications Union.

2. The data for Twitter and blog trends were collected by the Project on Information Technology and Political Islam. This project is among the first to analyze the flow of text messages about the potential and strategy of democratization movements among multiple countries. In addition, we figured out how to distinguish between domestic, regional, and international contributors to the growing online consciousness about political crisis. Demonstrating Twitter's impact on regional conversations is an important contribution but was technically challenging. We processed more than 3 million tweets for their use of hashtags about events in North Africa and the Middle East. We purchased cloud computing time from Amazon to speed up the text analysis, and wrote automated scripts for identifying the relevant tweets. A significant number of the tweets provide longitude and latitude information, and that information was automatically converted into country location. Finally, we hired a translator to help with texts and location information that is in Arabic, French, Hebrew, and Turkish.

   This dataset was created using the Twitter archiving service TwapperKeeper (http://twapperkeeper.com/) to capture the flow of tweets from the Twitter

Search API for Algeria, Egypt, Tunisia, Morocco, and Yemen. The hashtags analyzed, in order, were "#algeria," "#egypt," "#feb14," "#morocco," "#sidibouzid," and "#yemen." Since these archives were initiated by different users at different times, they do not all cover the same time period. The earliest, #sidibouzid, begins on January 14, 2011, and the last tweets (in multiple hashtags) occur on March 24, 2011. TwapperKeeper experienced system overloading at several times during this period, resulting in coverage gaps within some of the archives. But even for archives with no gaps, it is highly unlikely that TwapperKeeper's archive captured all relevant tweets due to limitations imposed by Twitter. All six archives combined contain a total of 3,142,621 tweets, some of which undoubtedly overlap because each tweet could contain multiple hashtags. More than 75 percent of these (2,363,139) are from #egypt. This method omits some unknown number of in-region tweeters due to blank location fields, deleted accounts, and garbled information in the fields.

Twitter changed its terms of service on March 20, 2011, to disallow public sharing of tweets. The archives analyzed in this report were queued for downloading from TwapperKeeper on March 19, 2011, but due to the backlog of similar requests from other users, the downloads did not become available until several days later (which is why some of them include tweets added after March 20). The archive dates for specific hashtags vary, and the earliest data points come from #egypt on January 5, 2011. All tracking ends March 20, 2011, due to Twitter's terms of service change. TwapperKeeper, the service used to track hashtags, was crippled (See www.readwriteweb.com/archives/how_recent_changes_to_twitters_terms_of_service_mi.php).

The hashtag archives included a wide array of metadata along with each tweet, including the author's name, the GMT it was posted, and the application used to send it, among other information. However, authors' self-reported location field was not included. To gather this, a list of unique users from each hashtag was created via a custom hypertext preprocessor (PHP) script. Each list was then used as an input into a second PHP script which automatically saved each user's location field from the Twitter REST API (representational state transfer application programming interface). Due to restrictions on the number of requests that can be sent to Twitter's REST API per hour, the user locations had to be collected one archive at a time. Location collection for the largest hashtags took longer than a day, with the exact amount of time depending on the number of unique users that contributed to it. Ultimately, between 25 percent and 40 percent of the unique users in each archive lacked any location data. Reasons for this included simply leaving the field blank, deleting one's account, or having it suspended due to misuse.

Once this script had finished collecting the location fields for all unique users from each hashtag archive, each data file was subjected to a word filter that attempted to automatically classify each user-provided location into one of four categories: (1) within the hashtag country; (2) within the broader Arabic region; (3) outside both the country and the Arabic region; and (4) no provided location. The first two filters consisted of a simple string-matching search pattern that sought the English name of each country along with the names of the top five cities by population in each country. The sole exception to this was for countries with less than 5 percent internet penetration, for which only the capital city was used in addition to the country name. Because many user-provided locations came in the form of latitude-longitude coordinates or were written in other languages, we decided to convert these into English before applying the filter. Google's reverse geocoding service was used for the former and Google Translate was used for locations written in Arabic script. Manually reading the translated locations, we were able to identify additional city names within the Arabic region that recurred often, so we added these to the word filter.

The procedure described here resulted in a dataset for each archive that consisted of each unique username and its category ID as determined by the word filter. To combine the category IDs with the full tweet data, each pair of archive files (consisting of one full tweet set and one list of unique names and category IDs) was loaded into a MySQL database hosted on a virtual Linux computer hosted by Amazon's commercial cloud. Custom structured query language (SQL) queries were used to automatically graft each unique user's location to each appearance of that user within the archive. Another SQL query tallied the number of tweets in each full archive classified as coming from a user in the hashtag country, in the broader Arabic region, outside of the country and region, and with no location. These summaries were aggregated by date and used to create time-series charts showing the posting dynamics of each location category.

3. The data for Figure 3.1 come from our analysis of the Tunisian blogosphere. This dataset was created using the eCairn Conversation archiving and analysis service. The tool was used to capture the flow of information through blog posts from Really Simple Syndication (RSS) feeds for Tunisia's key blogs. The captured data-streams begin on November 20, 2011, and end on May 15, 2011. A total of 475 key Tunisian blogs contributed a total of 26,000 posts during this period. A number of languages are represented in the Tunisian blogosphere, including Arabic, French, and English. We were able to analyze blog centrality through eCairn Conversation, and 17 of 475 blogs were identified as the main information gateways for the Tunisian blogosphere. In order of centrality, they are Tunisie Blogs; Wallada; Extravaganza; Tn-Bloggers; Boukornine; مدونة كاليمارو; Venus et Moi; Barbach; Tuniblogs; Notes; Carpe Diem; L'universe de Narwas; مياديــــن; Desenchantee; ولــد بيــــــرسا; Mon Massir; and Blogger. These 17 blogs (3.6 percent of the Tunisian national blogosphere) were linked to the remaining sphere of 475 blogs, of which 76

(16 percent) were located in a medium level of network centrality, 262 (55.1 percent) were in low network centrality; and 120 (25.2 percent) were network outliers and did not link to or share much dialogue with the rest of the Tunisian blogosphere.

Almost all of the 17 core blogs in the Tunisian blogosphere have been hosted within Tunisia. According to IP addresses, the cities of Tunis and al-Hammah have had the most prominent bloggers. The most central blogs in Tunis were El Fan, Tuniscope, and Tekino (all had medium network centrality in the larger Tunisian blogosphere). The most central blogs in al-Hammah were Tunisie Blogs, Tn-Bloggers, and Barbach (all had high network centrality in the larger Tunisian blogosphere). Interestingly, al-Hammah was a more critical location for the Tunisian blogosphere than Tunis. In addition, there have been several prominent Tunisian blogs maintained by people in the Tunisian diaspora. For example, the blogs Stupeur, Houblog, Arabasta, and Chroniques Absurdes were located in Montreal or Paris, belonged mostly to Tunisian expatriates, and were key mid-level blogs in the Tunisian national blogosphere.

The keywords identified for the analysis were determined using eCairn's conversation analyzer. The application used text search and identification algorithms to assess word frequencies and proximate phrases. This allowed us to specify Ben Ali, Bouazizi, Economie, Islam, Revolution, and Liberty as important conversation items in the Tunisian national blogosphere. After identifying important keywords, we reverse-analyzed their presence through time-series analysis. The discussion of Bouazizi and Liberty was consistently less frequent than other keywords, so were dropped from Figure 3.1. By sub-selecting the portions of the blogosphere that frequently mentioned different key words, we were able to investigate their particular network-structures. For example, the keywords appearing less frequently (e.g., Islam) had less network heterogeneity and were composed of less and mostly low-influence blogs. In contrast, blogs mentioning popular keywords (e.g., Revolution) had more network heterogeneity and were composed of larger, more diverse, and more high-level influence blogs driving those conversations. Put more simply, the networks of blogs within the Tunisian national blogosphere that were more diverse, cross-linked with others, and were key information gates were able to drive different topics of conversation more successfully than smaller and more homogeneous blog networks.

4. A comprehensive list of Egypt's political party and political pressure group data was built using both the Central Intelligence Agency's World Factbook, Wikipedia, and some specialized Egyptian political blogs anticipating that this combination of "official" and "unofficial" data could bring major and minor, new and established parties to the list. Several search engines and media databases were consulted to confirm the URLs for parties that had websites. In the pre-uprising dataset, a total of 1,332 external links were found across 10 active websites, of which 1,225 were unique and 102 were linked to by more than

one site. In the post-Mubarak dataset, a total of 927 external links were found across 9 active websites, of which, 828 were unique and 99 were linked to by more than one site. We searched for party websites in Arabic, in English transliterations of Arabic party names, and for the official English names of parties. To analyze the structure, the Web Data Extractor crawled each political party's URLs and extracted all external-facing URLs on the entire directory. All links from the first dataset were collected by the Web Data Extractor from November 11 to November 13, 2010, and all links from the second dataset were collected between May 3 and May 6, 2011. An XML based add-in for Microsoft Excel 2007 called NodeXL, developed by a team funded by Microsoft Research, was used to create network maps with the data like that pulled from the Web Data Extractor. NodeXL generated the Network Linkage Map between Political Parties in Egypt in Figures 3.3 and 3.4. An arrangement of nodes and clusters, the map is based on the Harel-Koren algorithm, which groups the nodes (individual sites as dots) based on common external links.

## Conclusion

1. The full dataset of all variables in the causal recipes described in this investigation is available at www.pITPI.org, as are the technical scripts for secondary solution sets not described here and the calibration points for specific membership sets.

# References

Abdul-Mageed, Muhammad M. 2008. "Online News Sites and Journalism 2.0: Reader Comments on Al Jazeera Arabic." *tripleC* 6(2): 59–76.

Aday, Sean, Henry Farrell, Marc Lynch, John Sides, John Kelly, and Ethan Zuckerman. 2010. *Blogs and Bullets: New Media in Contentious Politics.* Washington, DC: USIP. www.usip.org/publications/blogs-and-bullets-new-media-in-contentious-politics.

Al Jazeera English. 2009. "Al Jazeera Announces Launch of Free Footage under Creative Commons License." Press Release, January 13. http://cc.aljazeera.net/content/launch-press-release.

Al Nashmi, Eisa, Johanna Cleary, Juan-Carlos Molleda, and Melinda McAdams. 2010. "Internet Political Discussions in the Arab World: A Look at Online Forums from Kuwait, Saudi Arabia, Egypt and Jordan." *International Communication Gazette* 72(8): 719–38.

Al-Saggaf, Yeslam. 2004. "The Effect of Online Community on Offline Community in Saudi Arabia." *Electronic Journal of Information Systems in Developing Countries* 16(2): 1–16.

———. 2006. "The Online Public Sphere in the Arab World: The War in Iraq on the Al Arabiya Website." *Journal of Computer-Mediated Communication* 12(1): 311–34.

Anderson, Benedict. 1983. *Imagined Communities: Reflections on the Origin and Spread of Nationalism.* London, UK: Verso.

Anderson, Lisa. 2011. "Demystifying the Arab Spring: Parsing the Differences between Tunisia, Egypt, and Libya." *Foreign Affairs* 90(3): 2.

Andersson, Matilda, Marie Gillespie, and Hugh Mackay. 2010. "Mapping Digital Diasporas @ BBC World Service: Users and Uses of the Persian and Arabic Websites." *Middle East Journal of Culture and Communication* 3(2): 256–78.

Andrews, Robert. 2009. "Al Jazeera Offers Creative Commons Video, Lessig Lends Backing." *paidContent:UK*, January 14. http://paidcontent.org/tech/419-al-jazeera-offers-creative-commons-video-lessig-lends-backing/.

Ardalan, Davar. 2002. "Cyber Fatima, Muslim Women on the Web." *Islam on the Internet: Part II*. National Public Radio. www.npr.org/programs/watc/cyberislam/fatima.html.

Barkho, Leon. 2006. "The Arabic Al Jazeera vs. Britain's BBC and America's CNN: Who Does Journalism Right?" *American Communication Journal* 8(1): 1–15.

Bayat, Asef. 2007. *Making Islam Democratic: Social Movements and the Post-Islamist Turn*. Stanford, CA: Stanford University Press.

Bennett, W. Lance, and Alexandra Segerberg. 2012. "The Logic of Connective Action." *Information, Communication & Society* 15(5): 739–68. doi:10.1080/1369118X.2012.670661.

Bimber, Bruce A. 2003. *Information and American Democracy: Technology in the Evolution of Political Power*. Communication, Society and Politics. New York, NY: Cambridge University Press.

Bimber, Bruce, Andrew J. Flanagin, and Cynthia Stohl. 2005. "Reconceptualizing Collective Action in the Contemporary Media Environment." *Communication Theory* 15(4): 365–88.

Bosker, Bianca. 2011. "Al Jazeera Director General Wadah Khanfar Heralds 'Birth Of New Era' in Arab World." *Huffington Post*. www.huffingtonpost.com/2011/03/02/al-jazeera-wadah-khanfar_n_830318.html.

Brundidge, Jennifer, and Ronald E. Rice. 2009. "Political Engagement Online: Do the Information Rich Get Richer and the Like-minded More Similar?" In *The Handbook of Internet Politics*, ed. Phillip N. Howard and Andrew Chadwick. London, UK: Routledge.

Bureau of Democracy, Human Rights and Labor. 2005. "Libya." US Department of State. www.state.gov/g/drl/rls/hrrpt/2004/41727.htm.

Byrne, Dara N. 2007. "Public Discourse, Community Concerns, and Civic Engagement: Exploring Black Social Networking Traditions on BlackPlanet.com." *Journal of Computer-Mediated Communication* 13(1): 319–40.

Byrne, David, and Charles C. Ragin. 2009. *The SAGE Handbook of Case-based Methods*. Thousand Oaks, CA: Sage.

Camauer, Leonor. 2010. "Media Menus of Arabic Speakers: Stockholm." *Journalism* 11(6): 751–54.

Carr, Michelle, Sebrin Von Muellner, Triin Rum, and Jacob Sommer. 2011. "*The Construction of Identity by the Libyan Youth Movement on Facebook*." Uppsala, Sweden: Uppsala University.

Cheesman, Tom, Arnd-Michael Nohl, and BBC WS US Elections Study Group. 2011. "Many Voices, One BBC World Service? The 2008 US Elections, Gatekeeping and Trans-editing." *Journalism* 12(2): 217–33.

Converse, Philip E. 1987. "Changing Conceptions of Public Opinion in the Political Process." *Public Opinion Quarterly* 51(4): S12–S24.

Council on Foreign Relations, ed. 2011. *The New Arab Revolt: What Happened, What It Means, and What Comes Next*. Washington, DC: Council on Foreign Relations.

Dashti, Ali A. 2009. "The Role of Online Journalism in Political Disputes in Kuwait." *Journal of Arab & Muslim Media Research* 2(1–2): 91–112.

Deibert, Ronald J., John G. Palfrey, Rafal Rohozinski, and Jonathan Zittrain, eds. 2010. *Access Controlled: The Shaping of Power, Rights, and Rule in Cyberspace. Information Revolution and Global Politics.* Cambridge, MA: MIT Press.

———. 2008. *Access Denied: The Practice and Policy of Global Internet Filtering. Information Revolution and Global Politics.* Cambridge, MA: MIT Press.

DeLong-Bas, Natana J. ca. 2011. "The New Social Media and the Arab Spring." *Oxford Islamic Studies.* www.oxfordislamicstudies.com/Public/focus/essay0611_social_media.html.

Diamond, Larry J. 1994. "Toward Democratic Consolidation." *Journal of Democracy* 5(3): 4–17.

———. 2009. "Why Are There No Arab Democracies?" *Journal of Democracy* 21(1): 93–112. doi:10.1353/jod.0.0150.

Dickinson, Elizabeth. 2011. "The First Wikileaks Revolution?" *Foreign Policy*, January 13. http://wikileaks.foreignpolicy.com/posts/2011/01/13/wikileaks_and_the_tunisia_protests.

Dimitrova, Daniela V., and Colleen Connolly-Ahern. 2007. "A Tale of Two Wars: Framing Analysis of Online News Sites in Coalition Countries and the Arab World." *Howard Journal of Communications* 18(2): 153–68.

Dimitrova, Daniela V., Lynda Lee Kaid, Andrew Paul Williams, and Kaye D. Trammell. 2005. "War on the Web: The Immediate News Framing of Gulf War II." *International Journal of Press/Politics* 10(1): 22–44.

Dunn, Alexandra. 2010. "Public as Politician? The Improvised Hierarchies of Participatory Influence of the April 6th Youth Movement Facebook Group." Working paper. Cambridge, UK: Centre for Research in the Arts, Social Sciences and Humanities. www.polis.cam.ac.uk/cghr/docs/NMAP_Dunn_paper_4.pdf.

Earl, Jennifer, and Katrina Kimport. 2011. *Digitally Enabled Social Change: Activism in the Internet Age. Acting with Technology.* Cambridge, MA: MIT Press.

Eickelman, Dale F., and Jon W. Anderson. 2003. *New Media in the Muslim World: The Emerging Public Sphere.* 2nd ed. Indiana Series in Middle East Studies. Bloomington: Indiana University Press.

Etling, Bruce, John Kelly, Robert Faris, and John Palfrey. 2010. "Mapping the Arabic Blogosphere: Politics and Dissent Online." *New Media & Society* 12(8): 1225–43.

Fandy, Mamoun. 1999. "CyberResistance: Saudi Opposition between Globalization and Localization." *Comparative Studies in Society and History* 41(1): 24–47.

Friedman, Thomas. 2011 "Commencement Remarks to Tulane University." http://tulane.edu/grads/speakers-thomas-friedman.cfm.

Gallup. 2012. *After the Arab Springs: Women on Rights, Religion, and Rebuilding.* Washington, DC: Gallup Organization.

Gaouette, Brendan, and Nicole Greeley. 2011. "Untangling Dictators' Webs: The State Dept. Is Funding Tools to Help Online Activists Abroad." *BusinessWeek*, April 28. www.businessweek.com/magazine/content/11_19/b4227022810305.htm.

Garrett, R. 2006. "Protest in an Information Society: A Review of Literature on Social Movements and the New ICTs." *Information, Communication & Society* 9(2) (April): 202–24.

Garrett, R. Kelly. 2006. "Protest in an Information Society: A Review of Literature on Social Movements and the New ICTs." *Information, Communication & Society* 9(2): 202–24.

Gause, F. Gregory III. 2011. "Why Middle East Studies Missed the Arab Spring." *Foreign Affairs.* www.foreignaffairs.com/articles/67932/f-gregory-gause-iii/why-middle-east-studies-missed-the-arab-spring.

Ghareeb, Edmund. 2000. "New Media and the Information Revolution in the Arab World: An Assessment." *Middle East Journal* 54(3): 395–418.

Gladwell, Malcolm. 2010. "Small Change." *New Yorker,* October 4. www.newyorker.com/reporting/2010/10/04/101004fa_fact_gladwell.

Goldstone, Jack A. 2011. "Understanding the Revolutions of 2011." *Foreign Affairs.* www.foreignaffairs.com/articles/67694/jack-a-goldstone/understanding-the-revolutions-of-2011.

Hamdy, Naila. 2009. "Building Capabilities of Egyptian Journalists in Preparation for a Media in Transition." *Journal of Arab & Muslim Media Research* 1(3): 215–43.

Hidass, Ahmed. 2010. "Radio and Television in Morocco: New Regulation and Licensing for Private Channels." *Journal of Arab & Muslim Media Research* 3(1–2): 19–36.

Howard, Philip N. 2010. *Digital Origins of Dictatorship and Democracy: The Internet and Political Islam.* New York, NY: Oxford University Press.

Howard, Philip N., and Muzammil M. Hussain. 2011. "The Role of Digital Media." *Journal of Democracy* 22(3): 35–48.

Howard, Philip N., Sheetal D. Agarwal, and Muzammil M. Hussain. 2011. "When Do States Disconnect Their Digital Networks? Regime Responses to the Political Uses of Social Media." *Communication Review* 14(3): 216–32.

Howard, Philip N., Aiden Duffy, Deen Freelon, Muzammil Hussain, Will Mari, and Marwa Mazaid. 2011. *Opening Closed Regimes: What Was the Role of Social Media during the Arab Spring?* Seattle: University of Washington. www.pitpi.org.

Howard, Philip N., and Malcolm R. Parks. 2012. "Social Media and Political Change: Capacity, Constraint, and Consequence." *Journal of Communication* 62(2): 359–62. doi:10.1111/j.1460-2466.2012.01626.x.

Howard, Philip N., and World Information Access Project. 2007. *World Information Access Report 2007.* Seattle: University of Washington. www.wiaproject.org/index.php/191/2007-briefing-booklet.

Hussain, Muzammil M., and Philip N. Howard. 2012. "Opening Closed Regimes: Civil Society, Information Infrastructure, and Political Islam." In *Digital Media and Political Engagement Worldwide: A Comparative Study,* ed. Eva Anduiza, Michael J. Jensen, and Laia Jorba. Communication, Society and Politics. Cambridge, MA: Cambridge University Press.

el Issawi, Fatima, and Gerd Baumann. 2010. "The BBC Arabic Service: Changing Political Mediascapes." *Middle East Journal of Culture and Communication* 3(2): 137–51.

Jurkiewicz, Sarah. 2010. "Blogging as Counterpublic? The Lebanese and the Egyptian Blogosphere in Comparison." In *Social Dynamics 2.0: Researching Change in Times of Media Convergence*, ed. Nadja-Christina Schneider and Bettina Graf, 27–48. Berlin: Frank & Timme.

Khamis, Sahar. 2011. "The Transformative Egyptian Media Landscape: Changes, Challenges and Comparative Perspectives." *International Journal of Communication* 5: 1159–77.

King, Gary, Robert O. Keohane, and Sidney Verba. 1994. *Designing Social Inquiry: Scientific Inference in Qualitative Research*. Princeton, NJ: Princeton University Press.

Kloet, Jeroen. 2002. "Digitisation and Its Asian Discontents: The Internet, Politics and Hacking in China and Indonesia." *First Monday* 7(9). http://firstmonday.org/htbin/cgiwrap/bin/ojs/index.php/fm/article/viewArticle/1789/1669.

Kurzman, Charles. 1996. "Structural Opportunity and Perceived Opportunity in Social-Movement Theory: The Iranian Revolution of 1979." *American Sociological Review* 61(1): 153–70.

Labovitz, Craig. 2011. "Egypt Returns to the Internet." DDoS and Security Reports: The Arbor Networks Security Blog. http://ddos.arbornetworks.com/2011/02/egypt-returns-to-the-internet/.

Lee, Daniels. 2011. "Al Jazeera on Google TV." Corporate Blog. Google TV. http://googletv.blogspot.com/2011/02/al-jazeera-on-google-tv.html.

Lim, Merlyna. 2012. "Clicks, Cabs, and Coffee Houses: Social Media and Oppositional Movements in Egypt, 2004–2011." *Journal of Communication* 62(2): 231–48.

Lotan, Gilad, Erhardt Graeff, Mike Ananny, Devin Gaffney, Ian Pearce, and danah boyd. 2011. "The Revolutions Were Tweeted: Information Flows during the 2011 Tunisian and Egyptian Revolutions." *International Journal of Communication* 5: 1375–405.

Lynch, Marc. 2012. *The Arab Uprising: The Unfinished Revolutions of the New Middle East*. New York, NY: PublicAffairs.

———. 2006. *Voices of the New Arab Public: Iraq, Al-Jazeera, and Middle East Politics Today*. New York, NY: Columbia University Press.

Marcotte, Roxanne D. 2010. "Gender and Sexuality Online on Australian Muslim Forums." *Contemporary Islam* 4(1): 117–38.

Marks, Joseph. 2011. "Internet Repression on the Rise Since Arab Spring." *Nextgov*, July 15. www.nextgov.com/nextgov/ng_20110715_1793.php.

Marmura, Stephen. 2008a. "A Net Advantage? The Internet, Grassroots Activism and American Middle-Eastern Policy." *New Media & Society* 10(2): 247–71.

———. 2008b. "A Net Advantage? The Internet, Grassroots Activism and American Middle-Eastern Policy." *New Media & Society* 10(2) (April 1): 247–71.

Marshall, Monty G., and Keith Jaggers. 2010. *Polity IV: Political Regime Characteristics and Transitions, 1800–2009*. College Park, MD: Center for International Development and Conflict Management. www.systemicpeace.org/polity/polity4.htm.

McAdam, Doug. 1982. *Political Process and the Development of Black Insurgency, 1930–1970*. Chicago, IL: University of Chicago Press.

McLaughlin, W. 2003. "The Use of the Internet for Political Action by Non-state Dissident Actors in the Middle East (computer File)." *First Monday* (Online) 8(11) (November 3): 1.

McLaughlin, W. Sean. 2003. "The Use of the Internet for Political Action by Non-state Dissident Actors in the Middle East." *First Monday* 8(11). www.firstmonday.org/htbin/cgiwrap/bin/ojs/index.php/fm/article/viewArticle/1791.

Mellor, Noha. 2008. "Arab Journalists as Cultural Intermediaries." *International Journal of Press/Politics* 13(4): 465–83.

Mernissi, Fatema. 2004. "The Satellite, the Prince, and Scheherazade: The Rise of Women and Communicators in Digital Islam." *Transnational Broadcasting Studies* 12 (Spring). www.tbsjournal.com/Archives/Spring04/mernissi.htm.

Migdal, Joel S., Atul Kohli, and Vivienne Shue, eds. 1994. *State Power and Social Forces: Domination and Transformation in the Third World*. Cambridge Studies in Comparative Politics. Cambridge, UK: Cambridge University Press.

Miller, W. Flagg. 2007. *The Moral Resonance of Arab Media: Audiocassette Poetry and Culture in Yemen*. Harvard Middle Eastern Monographs. Cambridge, MA: Harvard Center for Middle Eastern Studies.

Morozov, Evgeny. 2011. *The Net Delusion: The Dark Side of Internet Freedom*. New York, NY: PublicAffairs.

Mourtada, Racha, and Fadi Salem. 2011. *Civil Movements: The Impact of Facebook and Twitter*. Arab Social Media Report. Dubai, UAE: Dubai School of Government. www.dsg.ae/en/Publication/Pdf_En/DSG_Arab_Social_Media_Report_No_2.pdf.

Nagel, Caroline, and Lynn Staeheli. 2010. "ICT and Geographies of British Arab, and Arab American Activism." *Global Networks* 10(2): 262–81.

Nagi, Eman Al, and Mohammad Hamdan. 2009. "Computerization and e-Government Implementation in Jordan: Challenges, Obstacles and Successes." *Government Information Quarterly* 26(4): 577–83.

Nisbet, Erik C., and Teresa A. Myers. 2010. "Challenging the State: Transnational TV and Political Identity in the Middle East." *Political Communication* 27(4): 347–66.

Noman, Helmi. 2011. *In the Name of God: Faith-based Internet Censorship in Majority Muslim Countries*. OpenNet Inititative. http://opennet.net/sites/opennet.net/files/ONI_NameofGod_1_08_2011.pdf.

Oghia, Michael J., and Helen Indelicato. 2011. "Ruling the Arab Internet: An Analysis of Internet Ownership Trends of Six Arab Countries." *Arab Media & Society* Summer (14). www.arabmediasociety.com/?article=779.

Papacharissi, Zizi, and Maria de Fatima Oliveira. 2012. "Affective News and Networked Publics: The Rhythms of News Storytelling on #Egypt." *Journal of Communication* 62(2): 266–82.

Pintak, Lawrence. 2009. "Border Guards of the 'Imagined' Watan: Arab Journalists and the New Arab Consciousness." *Middle East Journal* 63(2): 191–212.

Pintak, Lawrence, and Jeremy Ginges. 2008. "The Mission of Arab Journalism: Creating Change in a Time of Turmoil." *International Journal of Press/Politics* 13(3): 193–227.

Ragin, Charles C. 1987. *The Comparative Method: Moving beyond Qualitative and Quantitative Strategies*. Berkeley: University of California Press.

Rao, Madanmohan, ed. 2003. "Bangladesh." In *News Media and New Media: The Asia-Pacific Internet Handbook, Episode V*, 243–453. Communication & Media Studies. Singapore: Eastern Universities Press.

Relly, Jeannine E., and David Cuillier. 2010. "A Comparison of Political, Cultural, and Economic Indicators of Access to Information in Arab and non-Arab States." *Government Information Quarterly* 27(4): 360–70.

Robinson, John, Alan Neustadtl, and Meyer Kestnbaum. 2004. "Technology and Tolerance: Public Opinion Differences among Internet Users and Nonusers." In *Society Online: The Internet in Context*, ed. Philip N. Howard and Stephen Jones. Thousand Oaks, CA: Sage.

Rosenberg, Tina. 2011. "Friends in Revolution." *Opinionator*. http://opinionator. blogs.nytimes.com/2011/07/12/friends-in-revolution/.

Salamey, Imad, and Frederic S. Pearson. 2012. "The Collapse of Middle Eastern Authoritarianism: Breaking the Barriers of Fear and Power." *Third World Quarterly* 33(5): 931–48.

Saleh, Yasmine. 2011. "Social Media Show Limits as Egypt Elections Loom." *Reuters*. http://in.reuters.com/article/2011/07/20/idINIndia-58359520110720.

Sardar, Ziauddin. 1993. "Paper, Printing and Compact Disks: The Making and Unmaking of Islamic Culture." *Media, Culture & Society* 15(1): 43–59.

Seib, Philip M. 2008. *The Al Jazeera Effect: How the New Global Media Are Reshaping World Politics*. Washington, DC: Potomac Books.

Shumate, Michelle, and Jon Pike. 2006. "Trouble in a Geographically Distributed Virtual Network Organization: Organizing Tensions in Continental Direct Action Network." *Journal of Computer-Mediated Communication* 11(3): 802–24.

Slade, Christina. 2010. "Media and Citizenship: Transnational Television Cultures Reshaping Political Identities in the European Union." *Journalism* 11(6): 727–33.

Sreberny-Mohammadi, Annabelle, and Ali Mohammadi. 1994. *Small Media, Big Revolution: Communication, Culture, and the Iranian Revolution*. Minneapolis, MN: University of Minnesota Press.

Still, Brian. 2005. "Hacking for a Cause." *First Monday* 10(9). http://firstmonday.org/ htbin/cgiwrap/bin/ojs/index.php/fm/article/view/1274/1194.

Stowasser, Barbara. 2001. "Old Shaykhs, Young Women, and the Internet: The Rewriting of Women's Political Rights in Islam." *Muslim World* 91(1–2): 99–120.

Sullivan, Andrew. 2011. "Tunisia's Wikileaks Revolution." *Daily Beast*. http://andrewsullivan.thedailybeast.com/2011/01/tunisias-wikileaks-revolution.html.

Taylor, Chris. 2011. "Why Not Call It a Facebook Revolution?" *CNN Tech*, February 24. http://articles.cnn.com/2011-02-24/tech/facebook.revolution_1_facebook-wael-ghonim-social-media?_s=PM:TECH.

Tufekci, Zeynep, and Christopher Wilson. 2012. "Social Media and the Decision to Participate in Political Protest: Observations from Tahrir Square." *Journal of Communication* 62(2): 363–79.

Wright, Robin. 2011. "The Pink Hijab." *Wilson Quarterly*. www.wilsonquarterly.com/article.cfm?aid=1969.

Zayani, Mohamed. 2008. "The Challenges and Limits of Universalist Concepts: Problematizing Public Opinion in a Mediated Arab Public Sphere." *Middle East Journal of Communication and Culture* 1(1): 60–79.

# Index

CPSIA information can be obtained at www.ICGtesting.com
Printed in the USA
LVOW08s1914060913

351387LV00006B/11/P